Restitution

Restructuring School Discipline

Diane Chelsom Gossen

New View Publications
Chapel Hill

Restitution

Restructuring School Discipline

Cover illustration by Ranata Cardin

ISBN 0-944337-11-2

Library of Congress Catalog Card Number: 92-50360

Quantity Purchases
Companies, professional groups, clubs, and other organizations may
qualify for special terms when ordering quantities of this title. For
information contact the Sales Department, New View Publications,
P.O. Box 3021, Chapel Hill, N.C. 27515-3021.

Manufactured in the United States of America.

ACKNOWLEDGMENTS

I am indebted to my mentor Dr. William Glasser who first taught me Reality Therapy twenty-five years ago. His ideas have been an inspiration to me in the development of the philosophy of restitution.

Without Perry Good this book would not have been written. She encouraged me to put my ideas to paper, she critiqued me, and she worked closely with me on the final form as my publisher.

Several colleagues have over the years been instrumental to my ideas about changing the classroom. I acknowledge the contribution of Barnes Boffey, Shelley Brierley, Laurel Chelsom, Don Shinske, and also Richard Coutu who translated this material into French.

Over the past five years I have had the opportunity to work with several school districts. The people in these districts are integral to the ideas of this book. I thank Johnson City School District in New York, Sunnyside School District in Tucson, Arizona, S.E.R.E.S.C. Schools in New Hampshire, Tumwater School District in Washington, Quesnel School District in British Columbia, Lakeshore School District in Montreal and Le Phare in Quebec City.

This book was written with technical assistance from Jacqueline Eaton, who with her infinite patience exemplifies the practice of Control Theory.

A special thanks to the staff at New View Publications: Nancy Salmon edited the book, Rafaela Padilla did the desktop publishing, and Fred Good designed the cover. The children of Underwood Elementary School contributed the art work. Thanks to them, their art teacher, Debbie Jacobs, and their principal, Ann Dornan.

I would also like to thank Pam Martini for the valuable examples she provided.

Without my family I would not have been motivated to learn about "making it right." They have supported me in this project and have provided me with endless learning opportunities.

And above all I wish to acknowledge the parenting that I received from my parents, Elinor and Godfrey.

FOREWORD

My Evolution as an Educator

Nothing in the College of Education had prepared me to manage my students. I started my career as a teacher in 1960. I knew how to make lesson plans, how to print clearly on the chalkboard, and how to design tests. Curriculum was my main focus. Getting the right answer was the key. I had not learned, however, how to make the classroom need-fulfilling for my students. My teacher behaviors actually disrupted the students' needs. I said things like, "No laughing," "No talking," "You're wrong." When I had difficulty with a student, instead of increasing involvement with him, I ignored him or gave him judgmental looks. As a last resort I sent one of my students for corporal punishment from the principal. Conformity was my goal. I was not happy in this job.

Ten years later, inspired by a course on Reality Therapy with William Glasser, I piloted an alternate education program in my home town of Saskatoon, Saskatchewan. This program operated from an individually focused, open education philosophy. Gone was corporal punishment. We were idealistic advocates for our students against the system.

Later, as a faculty member in the College of Education, I conducted many in-service training sessions for teachers. They learned how to establish reasonable rules and consequences, and they learned to do class meetings. Although the students were attentive in the class meetings, they remained unmotivated for many of the core subject lessons. When the teachers used motivational techniques, the class was temporarily involved but so often the students seemed to have no real joy in learning. I became discouraged and didn't work in schools for five more years. I had no answer. I abandoned my first profession.

In the 1980's I trained mainly in the areas of corrections and addictions — where the real action was. Over and over again in each of these settings the group directed discussions back to the client's history of school failure. I concurred, shrugged my shoulders and commented that this was why I had left Education. I was what I would term deeply discouraged. I believe I was representative of many others who had begun to teach on the crest of the individualism of the late 1960's. I knew I had skills, I genuinely liked kids, but the obstacles seemed insurmountable.

In 1981 I began a kind of learning which I had never experienced before. William Glasser introduced me to the work of control theorist William Powers. Studying the model of a self-regulating system as set out in *Stations of the Mind* resulted in a major paradigm shift for me. I began to teach the principles of internal motivation.

In 1987 I was drawn back into the field of Education by an invitation from the Johnson City Schools to teach Control Theory to their administrators. As I worked with this group, I recognized a process very different from that to which I was accustomed. As I presented the Control Theory concepts, I was continuously stopped and questioned. The participants spoke both to me and across me as they integrated what I taught with the goals of their program. As I interacted with the group I felt optimism begin to grow within me.

The Johnson City Schools epitomized the philosophy of quality in education. They celebrated the student as an individual. They had a no-fail academic program. For seven years they had been using the questions of Reality Therapy on themselves, their teachers, and their students. Spending time in these schools, I recognized that the teachers and students had the strong sense of ownership of their program that was necessary to be successful.

In 1988 Dr. Glasser introduced the Deming Model, combining it with Reality Therapy and Control Theory into the discussion of school change. Here was what I had been waiting for. Here was the theory that explained to me what was happening in Johnson City.

Too often schools operate with an ineffective management model. Applying W.E. Deming's principles to school management, using the ideas of the Quality School, enabled me to analyze why previous school change had been transitory, why Johnson City Schools were so successful. It became clear to me that the discipline model used by most schools focused on the misdemeanor rather than on helping the child learn a better way to behave. As I thought about it, it also became clear that a better way not only made a reparation for a wrong, but it strengthened the child. It could be used to make an amend to an individual. It could be used to help the child become a more socially responsible member of the group. Such a principle could be used in mastery learning to encourage students to retest on exams to challenge themselves. The concept of restitution as a vehicle for the child to grow and learn appealed to me.

OVERVIEW

The concept of restitution can be used to restructure schools away from traditional methods of discipline. Restitution is not retribution. Restitution provides the teacher with a process to redirect the individual. In the restitution model the teacher's actions do not diminish the individual. Rather, the teacher uses restitution as a tool to gain control without sacrificing the self-esteem of the individual. When students understand that the goal of discipline is to strengthen them and to teach them, they will no longer be afraid to face their mistakes. They will begin to view a problem as an opportunity for learning a better way.

Since 1990 schools have been actively pursuing restructuring. Al Shankar says of restructuring, "Minor changes will not bring about the improvements we need in schools ... Changes have to be major, the kind of changes that take place in a factory when they move away from the assembly line model."

In the process of restructuring school discipline it is imperative for our movement toward change to be based on research. Research is telling us that the methods we have been using to manage students are not working. Research is validating the importance of intrinsic motivation. Research is indicating the short-term success of extrinsic motivation. Furthermore, research is telling us that extrinsic motivation tends to decrease intrinsic motivation. Our attempts to reinforce children's appropriate behavior extrinsically and to control their misbehavior externally do not work for very long.

The thesis of this book is that teaching students to make restitution rather than applying consequences externally will get us the change we want in the schools. Our established practices of managing people tend to train them to focus externally on evaluation of their faults by others. The restitution approach assists people in making an internal evaluation of what they can do to repair their mistakes. This approach is consistent with the theory of man as a self-regulating system. We have the knowledge of internal motivation available in Control Theory. As set out by William Powers in *Behavior: The Control of Perception* and by William Glasser in *Control Theory*, this theory is consistent with the beliefs of outcome-based education. Based on a theory of human needs, it is supported by twenty-five years of implementation of Reality Therapy. This book presents ideas for actions that teachers can take to get the long-term effects they desire with students.

Discipline is the workshop topic most sought after by teachers. Teachers say that if the children would only behave, they could help them to learn. They want to know techniques to apply to a classroom to curtail disruptions. Teachers report that discipline is the most challenging part of their job.

What is it that makes discipline such a burden? Is discipline the responsibility of the teacher? Should supervisors be evaluating teachers on their ability to discipline children? Have parents the right to ask the teacher to discipline their child?

Let us look at the word discipline. It is derived from the Latin word *disciplina*, which means learning. The verb *discipline* comes from the same root as the word *disciple*. The original meaning of this word connotes the self-discipline necessary to master a task. This is the self-discipline of the students of Socrates and Plato, of the competitive athlete, of the "Karate Kid". Self-discipline allows a person to harness his potential towards a goal, toward what he values. In our culture we have transformed the meaning of discipline into something one does to another to encourage conformity. We tend to associate the word discipline with discomfort, not with what we value.

This book is an attempt to rediscover the true meaning of discipline. The goal of any intervention should be to assist the student in developing self-discipline. This book proposes a restructuring of classroom management toward a principle called restitution. Restitution, the creative part of self-discipline, is the key to a constructive, humane approach for guiding children. A child can learn to remedy his mistakes. A child can be assisted to make reparations. We don't focus on the fault or the mistake. We focus on making things right.

Contents

"Rewards and punishments
are the lowest form
of education."
— *Chuang-tzu*

Chapter One

Current Discipline Practices

When teachers are in a position of authority over others, they can relate to those they manage from several different positions. These positions are familiar and you may recognize yourself as you move up and down the scale. In the first four positions the teacher is trying to be in control. In the fifth choice the teacher, as Manager, practices restitution which leads to self-discipline.

Failure < —————————————————— > Success

Punisher • Guilter • Buddy • Monitor • Manager

Punisher

This person punishes and may use anger, criticism, humiliation, or corporal punishment. The old-time severe schoolmaster is an example of this approach. He says, "Do it or else!"

Guilter

The person in this position uses silence, withdrawal of approval, remarks that instill guilt, or moralizing to punish. The stereotype of the long-suffering mother who says "It's alright, just leave me behind," is an example. The Guilter says, "Why didn't you do what you should have done?"

Buddy
This person uses friendship and humor to influence the person he supervises. Although this approach doesn't harm the recipient, it can lead to dependency as the recipient complies for the other. Also, it is very hard for the recipient to build a strong internal locus of control and sense of responsibility. There can also be resentment toward the "Buddy" who has to discipline. The person says to the Buddy, "I thought you were my friend!" This position is not bad, but it has its limits in terms of helping a person develop independence. The buddy says, "Do it for me!"

Monitor
This person uses stimulus-response discipline, meting out consequences, either positive or negative. The person being disciplined does learn by this approach that society has rules and limits. If the supervisor is consistent, the recipient learns to conform to avoid discomfort. However, this approach becomes boring. After awhile the recipient learns ways to get around the system, or may decide to be unreceptive to the rewards or consequences. An example of this system is the Assertive Discipline approach. The Monitor says, "You have earned ten check marks," or "You have lost 15 minutes of free time."

These four choices of control encompass most of the current discipline procedures used in schools. The first three are dependent on the student-teacher interaction. The fourth is usually the policy a school has developed, setting out a series of escalating consequences.

Punishment and guilt are derived from the hierarchical parental model where children are viewed as extensions of ourselves. The Buddy and the Monitor understand that children have separate control systems, but believe children can be controlled externally.

The first two positions, punishment and guilt, are based on negative control, whereas the Buddy and the Monitor exert positive control. The Manager on the other hand, encourages self-control.

Manager

The Manager may use the Monitor or Buddy approach as a fall-back position, but prefers to focus on restitution first. The recipient of this approach has to work hard to figure out an appropriate pay-back for his irresponsible behavior. The emphasis is not on the offender receiving a consequence, but rather on his compensating the victim. The Manager says, "How are you going to make things right? When can you do it?"

Who Would Say...?

- I'm disappointed in you. (*Guilter*)

- You never get it right. (*Punisher*)

- Do it for me. (*Buddy*)

- Do you want a happy face sticker today? (*Monitor*)

- Didn't you say you'd do it? (*Guilter*)

- You're always the last one to finish. (*Punisher*)

- How can you make it better? (*Manager*)

- You won't get a star if you don't finish. (*Monitor*)

- How many times have I told you? (*Guilter*)

- Remember what I did for you? (*Buddy*)

- You'll never get anywhere in life. (*Punisher*)

- What's your plan to fix it? (*Manager*)

The Illusions of Control

In order for teachers to become Managers, they must discard several common, deeply ingrained misconceptions. These are:

I. The Illusion that We Can Control the Student

In fact, we can't force anyone to do something he doesn't choose to do. Even when it appears we are controlling a student's behavior he is allowing us to control him, because at the moment it is his most need-fulfilling choice.

II. The Illusion that All Positive Reinforcement Works and is Beneficial

Positive reinforcement or persuasion is controlling. Any attempt to influence a student through praise to repeat a behavior is an attempt to control him. After awhile the student begins to recognize this and resists our attempts, or he may become dependent on the teacher's opinion of his efforts.

III. The Illusion that Criticism and Guilt Build Character

Using miserable behaviors to control children leads to their developing a failure identity. They learn to feel badly about themselves. They develop negative self-talk. Sometimes it is hard for teachers to recognize themselves using guilt, because often it is only their tone of voice that conveys the guilt message.

IV. The Illusion that Adults Have the Right to Coerce Children

Adults believe that they have the responsibility to make children do certain things. Whatever it takes is acceptable if it results in measurable performance improvement.

Let's look at each of these illusions in greater depth.

I. The Illusion that We Can Control the Student

Teachers believe they can control students. Consider Ken. He simply refused to cooperate. He chose to not follow school rules, and he did not care whether or not he stayed in school. He answered in the negative to questions such as "Is it important to pass your grade?" "Do you care what the kids think of you?" "If you do nothing, will it get better?" I had the urge to coerce Ken, to debate his perception, to threaten him with failure in school, in life. However, I was able to remain calm, state our desire to work it out, and state what our position would be if he chose not to follow the rules. I was even able to use a bit of humor. When Ken remained not ready to change, however, I as his teacher had to recognize it. He was not ready to be learning in the class at this time.

A teacher can use all these questions and can gain involvement, but if a student insists on a certain path, we'd best let him reap the consequences of his decision. If we persuade him or threaten him we have responsibility for his choice. Students will attempt to have us take responsibility for their learning. We need to establish with each class our refusal to absolve the student of responsibility for his own decisions with regard to learning.

How Can I Control You?

As the teacher of an eighth grade class I might ask, "What do you think my job is?" They would usually answer, "To teach us." If I am lucky they will answer, "To make us learn." I say lucky because this would mean they are putting the coercion issue on the table right away. If they don't say this I will ask, "Do you think I can make you learn what I have to teach?" I'll even personalize it. I'll ask the class, "Suppose I want Darin to learn the states of the former Soviet Union. How will I make him learn these?" The students might say, "Make it interesting." I can answer, "I will try to do that, but suppose I do and he doesn't want to learn. How will I make him learn these?" They might say, "Bribe him." I'll answer, "I could do that, maybe offer him free time for learning. But if he doesn't want what I have to offer, can I make him learn this?" Inevitably the suggestion of detention will arise, then the vice principal's office and even suspension. My question remains the same. If we do all these things and he doesn't want to put this information in his head, can I make him learn? Undiscouraged, the class will suggest phoning his parents. Together we explore a variety of sanctions they might invoke including kicking him out. The question remains, "Suppose they do all these things and he doesn't want to say what we want him to say, can we make him do it?"

Undeterred, someone will say, "Put a gun to his head. Then he'll learn." Wearily I retort, "But if we do that and he really believes that what he wants is more important than what we want him to do, ... if he is willing to forfeit his life, can we make him learn, say, or do anything he doesn't want to do?" At this point the students tend to agree that we could not make him accept our agenda if he's willing to pay the ultimate price. This is an opportunity to review history, especially recent history. I ask the students if they know of any examples where people threatened with survival have decided to assert their free will. "What about the Chinese man who confronted the tanks in Tienamen Square? What about the grandmother in Moscow who called up to the tank operator saying, 'You can't do this; we raised you'? What about the people in Romania who locked arms in front of their church? What about the teenagers of Timor who were murdered this past November?" And then there is Joan of Arc and Copernicus and Malcolm X and the Buddhist monks who self-immolate. My question remains, "If a person doesn't want to do what I want him to do, can I make him do it?"

I tell the students that I refuse to put coercion in my job description, because I don't believe I can meet a commitment to make anyone do anything. It is not my job. My job is to offer information, to offer examples, to answer questions, to demonstrate, to explore, to question. It is the students' job to learn if they decide it is what they want.

What Do You Think?

Discuss these questions with a colleague or with your principal.

- Whose job is it to learn?

- Is it our job to motivate the students? Or is it our job to provide a safe non-judgmental environment in which they can motivate themselves?

- Is it our job to make our students learn? Or is it our job to create the conditions for learning and is it the students' job to learn?

- Is it our job to make students be nice to each other? Or is it our job to model awareness of other's needs, kindness, acceptance?

- Is it our job to make the students follow the rules? Or is it our job to tell them what we are obligated to do if they don't do their job in keeping their commitment to what the group has decided?

II. The Illusion that All Positive Reinforcement Works and is Beneficial

A young child behaves without passing judgment on himself. If we routinely supply positive reinforcement for that which we want to see more, after awhile the child doesn't feel complete unless he hears our approval after each of his performances. Eventually, however, the need for freedom of expression becomes greater than the needs for power and belonging, and the child refuses to meet our agenda. Sometimes we then decide that we can only help by coercing the child through negative actions.

How do we engage children in a cycle of positive reinforcement? Consider the child who comes to school for the first time. His parents have told him the teacher is important. He has already been socialized to consider her a significant other. Therefore her comments will be important to him.

Imagine the first day of school when children are offered the option to do free drawing. The teacher observes a child; let's name him Peter. She notices he is making an attractive border on his picture, and she is pleased. What behaviors do you think she will use?

The odds are she will say something about his drawing such as, 'I really like that, Peter. I especially think you've done a beautiful job with your decoration on the sides.' She may even hold up his work and show the rest of the class his innovation. Peter may smile or be shy, but Peter will likely feel happy with the comment. So, what do you think the teacher will see on his next picture?

Although Peter drew without self-consciousness the first day, what might we expect him to do the second day as the teacher passes? Perhaps look over his shoulder? Point to his picture? Hold it up and beckon her? What does he want to hear? What is happening in this interaction? Is Peter now internally or externally directed? Whose opinion of his work does he consider paramount? His or the teacher's?

The question is, would Peter have cared if on the first day the teacher had said 'Oh' and passed on? Would it have been a negative experience for him, or would it have passed unnoticed without influencing his output?

I am not saying we as teachers should totally resist positive reinforcement. It is too difficult and may not even be desirable. What I am saying, however, is that we need to be aware that our compliments are shifting the child from self-control and self-directed behavior to external control and compliance.

Do we believe that children are intrinsically motivated by innate curiosity and a desire to learn about everything in our environment? Are we aware of the incredible potency of this inner drive? If so, we need to re-examine our belief in praise and rewards.

Dreikurs partially understood this. He wrote of the need to switch from praise to encouragement. He understood that praise was our commentary on the end product, and he encouraged us to comment instead on the effort the child was putting forth. Thousands of teachers have implemented this suggestion with positive results.

What I am asking here is for us to consider the value of refraining from commenting so extensively on the performance of the children in our charge. We need to understand that any control by us, even positive control, can influence the child's ability to meet his needs. An example would be if we are on the golf course with a partner and we comment on his score and say, "That's great. How did you do that?" He begins to focus on our comment rather than on his effort. Another example is when a person doing creative work is reluctant to show it to anyone because a comment might dictate further efforts.

Let's continue with the story of Peter. Suppose Peter gets tired of doing borders. The compliments have been nice, but after awhile he'd rather do his pictures as he wishes, or perhaps not do one at all. What will happen? Picture this scene.

The teacher is passing down a row of children. She is praising them for their work, smiling, complimenting, and displaying what she views. As she reaches Peter's desk she sees a blank paper. She says "Hum" in a perfunctory manner, then turns quickly to the next student lifting his completed work to demonstrate enthusiastically for the group an on-task effort. What will the other students do? What will Peter do? What

are his choices? Will he quickly pick up his pencil?
Will he put his head down? Will he rip up his paper?
Or something else?

I ask you this question, "Would Peter have been upset
if the teacher had leaned over his shoulder the first
day and said, 'hum.' If she had never established the
conditions for reinforcement in the first place would
he care whether or not he heard a comment from her?
Would he be waiting for her approval, or would he be
content with his own progress?

This story illustrates how positive reinforcement cre-
ates the conditions for a child to feel badly if the approval is held back. We condition him to hearing a
positive reinforcement so that when he hears nothing
he may be disconcerted. This pattern may result
either in his conformity or his rebellion.

Now you will say, "We are not automatons! We are
human beings with feelings of our own, both positive
and negative.' You may ask, "Are we to refrain from
spontaneous expression?" The answer is, of course, no.
Keep what is spontaneous, for it is a natural compo-
nent of your behavior. If you suddenly see something
exceptional, it will be normal for your face and your
voice to reflect this. For example, if students make a
surprise card for a teacher returning from sick leave
she might exclaim, 'I love it! It's beautiful!' If I return
home to find my teenager has unexpectedly cleaned
his room I may shriek in delight, 'Right on, Jake!' Such
outbursts are not purposefully planned to motivate a
repetition of the behavior. I did not think before I ex-

claimed 'Right on.' My pleasure was a spontaneous part of my total behavior.

This is different from a teacher's or parent's calculated reinforcement of a behavior to ensure its repetition. We teachers spend a large part of our day, especially in the primary grades, making positive statements about children's on-task behaviors. Sometimes we do this so often that the energetic cheerful output drains us. It takes a great deal of energy to attempt to motivate other people. Even when students appear to welcome positive reinforcements, continuously supplying them is a drain on the energy we need for teaching. Some days we drag ourselves home exhausted. Is this familiar?

The majority of children we teach come to us from a culture that rewards positive behaviors and punishes negative behaviors. They come to us already inured in a system of rewards, treats, hugs, pats, smiles and many comments linked to their performance. They expect this. They watch us to see what reward system we will choose. They observe us to see how they can control us by understanding the goal of our intent. They are masters at figuring this out. Just as they have learned to get what they want from each of their parents in different ways, they will get what they want from us. They need only observe and listen as we lay out the conditions for reinforcement and identify what we want to see. They are finely tuned and heed us and our expectations because years of experience have taught them that they can comply, negotiate, and manipulate to get what they want. If you doubt this, just observe a four-year-old playing teacher as she metes out rewards and sanctions to her friends.

When we reward the students we get the behavior and work output we believe are important. We may in fact be limiting the output the students feel is important to them.

After awhile the rewards begin to lose their effectiveness. Classrooms which have adopted the Assertive Discipline program also discovered this. The first year the program worked beautifully. The children knew where they stood and performed for the rewards. By the second year, the rewards had to be varied and more elaborate in order to hold their interest. Mostly, more and more negative sanctions were being used. Pizza parties lost their novelty and budgets were being overdrawn. Sometimes the teachers felt like punishing and often they resorted to guilt because they felt the children had violated their covenant. The children no longer wanted to be controlled. One teacher gave out five-cent, miniature chocolate bars to students who earned a certain number of points. A difficult student worked hard for the bars for a while. But eventually he started to bring his own sixty-cent chocolate bars to school and refused to work.

This leaves us with a dilemma. How can we move students who have been socialized into a positive reinforcement cycle to the stage beyond dependence on our reinforcement? Is it possible for children who have been in a stimulus-response reward system to move toward internal motivation and evaluation? I believe it is.

Giving up chosen calculated positive reinforcement is the hardest thing teachers have to do. If the child has heard only negatives, he needs to hear positives, but mostly he needs to hear himself saying them to himself. In any training workshop I like to begin monitoring the number of times we use the word 'good." We are indiscriminate. It can mean many things, from 'I like it," to 'I've heard enough of that! Close it off." Ask the people with whom you work to begin explaining what they mean when they use the word 'good."

Almost any time that we are saying the word 'good" without a strong positive burst of feeling, we are using it to control someone. This action on our part needs to be continuously evaluated. We need to ask ourselves, 'Is this helping a child build a strong internal locus of control? Is he learning to evaluate his own performance and to reward himself for a quality job?"

What Can We Do?

1. Keep expressing positive emotions that we feel.

2. Build self-evaluation. Ask the child, "What do you like about what you did? What was easy? What was hard? How did you figure it out?"

3. Build self-esteem. Ask children, "What do you give yourself credit for? What did work?"

4. Validate the misbehavior. With regard to an identified negative trait say, "You don't have that behavior for no reason. You learned it a long time ago and it has helped you. You'll always know how to do this, but can you figure out another way that works just as well and doesn't cause a problem for other people?"

5. When giving feedback on performance be sure to start with "I".

   - I learned from this ...
   - I appreciated from you ...
   - I was interested in ...

III. The Illusion that Guilt and Criticism Build Character

I have found that many teachers choose to focus on a child's past inadequacies and insist that his previous poor performance must be reflected in his score as a reminder to him. They also like to use a certain tone of voice to remind the child of his failed promises and his unmet aspirations. They believe criticism is their right and their responsibility. They believe this method is necessary for the child to learn to be a success. This premise works with some children, but as Glasser points out in *Schools Without Failure*, it only works for children who have experienced the success side. It doesn't work for children with a failure identity.

Sometimes when I am working with a school district, a board member will question the shift from punishment to discipline. He may say, 'My father was tough on us, and I'm a better person for it.' In this kind of situation I have learned to ask, 'Did you know your parents loved you? Did your father teach you things that have helped you in life?' The answer has always been, 'Yes.' Then I tell them, 'You are a successful person. Punishment does work on successful people because they can absorb it and forgive the Punisher. Punishment does not work on a child who has a failure identity because this course of action merely confirms his inadequacy.'

Teachers experiment with various ways of controlling classes. When, as a new teacher, I feared I was losing control, I yelled and punished like the teachers I had learned from in my own school days. I realized, however, if I didn't change that pattern, my supervisor would not give me a good evaluation. So I shifted from the critical position to the guilting position. I lowered my voice. I told the students how disappointed I was in them. I pointed out that they could be doing better, and then I asked why they had fallen short in their performance. I remained in control of my own emotions at the same time as I manipulated the children's feelings. As a result a child felt badly but was inclined to conform to my expectations. Although they conformed, I took no real satisfaction, because it was clear to me their conformity was at the expense of their self-esteem. I realized that guilt was contributing to the children's failure identity.

As a parent and then as a teacher, I can recall taking satisfaction in the visible upset of the child who had erred. I said to myself, 'Good, she knows she has done wrong.' I harbored the illusion that this recognition on her part was an end in itself. Seldom did I actively seek to relieve this discomfort by helping the child remedy the situation. More often an apology was accepted or sometimes extracted.

What do we accomplish if we leave a person feeling guilty and devalued? Do we do this to feel superior? Has the concept of penance influenced us?

Think again of the child's face before you. She knows she's made a mistake. She feels guilty, perhaps even defensive. How do you want her to feel? Wretched, worthless, miserable? Or do you want her to have the opportunity to regain her lost self-esteem? You have a choice. You can focus on the misdemeanor, or you can focus on the restitution.

Suppose I ask you now to write down without looking back the four illusions stated at the beginning of this chapter. After doing this, check your answers and give yourself a score. Then review the illusions and take a retest. Finally, I ask you to consider both tests and give yourself a final score. What is your real score on this test?

How much of that material do you now understand? (100%) What amount of the knowledge on this test had you mastered ten minutes ago, before reviewing? Did your first score reflect this? What have you mastered now? Does your second score reflect this? Do you believe that your earned score should be an average of the two scores? Do you believe that if you got two out of four correct on the first test (50%) and four out of four correct in the second test (100%) your legitimate score is 75%? Do you think that there will be no motivation for you to get it right the first time if you have too many chances to do it over? How would you feel if we posted your average score? How would you feel if we posted your best final score? Which feedback from the world would be more motivating?

IV. The Illusion that Adults Have the Right to Coerce

How does one coerce someone else? Coercion is a strong word. It means to compel by force. Few of us would wish to admit we use coercion, especially when we speak of the adult-child relationship. To compel by force. The question is, "By what force?" Force can be defined as energy, power, vigor, or strength. Force can mean violence. Force can also mean the power to convince or persuade.

We adults compel children by the force of our convictions. We attempt to persuade them that one course of action is better than another. We may do this in a friendly manner, such as 'C'mon, you'll really be happy when it's finished,' or 'Please, do it for me.' When this is ineffective we may add a dash of guilt, such as, 'Didn't you say you were going to do this?' or 'Don't you think you should do better?' If these approaches do not convince the child, we may progress to threats of confinement or loss of privilege. Some adults may coerce with warnings of physical harm; others carry out these threats through violence.

Most of us, at one time or another, have used all of these tactics on the children in our care. In fact, some school divisions still allow the use of corporal punishment. For them, the teacher is viewed as a reasonable and just parent surrogate, and a reasonable and just parent has the right to spank a child. How much do we sanction coercion of children in our society?

Some societies have drawn a clear legal line. In Scandinavia laws have been passed that forbid any adult to hit a child. The child has the right to be safe and to be respected. A child can report his or her parents. When I went down the street with my three-year-old in Bergen, Norway, and he collapsed, choosing not to cooperate, I gave him a gentle swat on the bottom. Alarmed, my sister said, "Don't do that! You could be arrested! Someone will come up to you and say something!" Are we ready for such a stand in North America?

In the last decade professionals have been required to report cases of abuse. How severe must abuse be before it is reported? Is it different in cities or rural areas, north or south? What's our standard?

What do you believe about the right of an adult to coerce a child by physical means? How much force would you observe an adult use on a child in a grocery store before you would intervene? What would you do if the parent yelled at the child? If he or she swore or verbally castigated the child, what would you do? If the parent shook the child, would you intervene? How hard would the shaking need to be? How many times have you intervened when a child is slapped? How many times would you tolerate this? If a child is hit with a closed fist, would that bring you to his rescue? Would his age make a difference?

Try asking your friends these questions. If nothing else, try to answer them for yourself. In answers to my questioning, I have experienced the whole continuum.

One man said he intervened once when an adult pushed a child's face against the sidewalk. A woman said that when a child is being severely rebuked she goes and stands silent witness to the scene and it generally deters the adult. The most common response to my questions is silence.

What does this mean? Does it mean we do not witness such events in public places? Does it mean people are thinking of an answer? What does this silence say about our society? Does the silence reflect our attitude to compelling by force, one person to another? Is it because the example deals with a child in care of an adult? Has the child fewer rights? Is the child an unruly appendage, a possession to be disciplined, controlled? Where do we draw the line?

Summary

There are five positions we can take in our attempt to control children. We are Punishers when we hurt them, criticize them, or humiliate them. We are Guilters when we focus on the past, on their mistakes, and on broken promises. We can act as the Buddy and positively control them with compliments, smiles, and praise. As Monitors, we reward their good behavior and withhold privileges when they don't comply with what we want. Lastly we act as a Manager when we teach them to make restitution for mistakes and to make reparations to the group.

Let us re-examine the illusions we adults harbor with regard to discipline in light of the basic psychological needs which Dr. William Glasser believes all people have. They are: love or belonging, power or importance, fun or pleasure, and freedom.

1. The first illusion is that we can control another: In terms of the psychological needs this belief gives us a sense of personal power, but it interferes with another's freedom.

2. The second illusion is that all positive reinforcement is beneficial: Positive reinforcement can give us control as well as create belonging with the student. The problem is that it can interfere with a child's locus of control. It can also result in a loss of freedom for us, as children require a constant infusion of positive comments from us.

3. The illusion that guilt and criticism help children: Guilt and criticism may give us temporary control. The danger is that they can harm our belonging with the other person. The child may decide to exclude us as a significant other if the pain is too great for him. Also, learning cannot be fun in an environment where students fear censure.

4. The fourth illusion is that adults have the right to coerce: The view that adults have of children as personal property gives them a sense of power. However, children begin to resist this concept as they mature. In the teenage years the child's growing need for freedom and the adult's desire to keep control can result in open conflict. Many adults have said they stopped punishing their child when he became big enough to fight back.

"Where does discipline end?
Where does cruelty begin?
Somewhere between these,
thousands of children
inhabit a voiceless hell."
— *Francois Mauriac*

Chapter Two

Control Me If You Can

The Differences Between Discipline and Punishment

What are the differences between discipline and punishment? Discipline is reasonable in the eyes of those who receive it and in the eyes of society as a whole. It is expected; the rules are known by all and are consistently enforced. It leads, at best, to the child making a reparation, or perhaps, to his receiving a natural or logical consequence. The goal of good discipline is always to avoid a similar problem in the future by the child's learning a better behavior. Good discipline generally results in a better relationship between the adult and the child. No child will say at the moment he is being disciplined, "Thank you very much, I know this will make me a better person." But, after a period of time, up to twenty-four hours, the relationship will be stronger because the child knows our limits, and when calmed down, he can recognize his part in the problem. An example of this is when a class has been pushing the teacher for limits and the teacher clamps down. There is a relaxation that ensues as the students recognize the teacher can take control if necessary.

Discipline may be externally imposed or may be manifest as self-discipline. In order for an interaction to qualify as discipline, whatever happens must be expected. The child must know the rule and have seen it applied to others in similar situations. Therefore, when the child errs, he knows something will consistently happen. In order for an action to be good discipline, it must also be reasonable. It cannot be excessive. Only the minimum amount of intervention is used to change behavior. Discipline is also best done without negative emotion. It needs to be calm, relevant, and non-critical. The more forceful the intervention, the more the adult needs to be in control of his or her feelings.

In management that is less coercive, awareness of the tone of voice is crucial in that it carries approximately one-third of the message. The words are a mere 10%. More than half of the message is conveyed in the nonverbal expressions of the face and the body. Think for a moment of the many ways one might transmit the question, "What's the rule?" We could interrogate, be sarcastic, kind, playful, or guilting. Each message will elicit from the child a different response. It is not what is said that is so important, but how it is said. Any approach to managing can be perverted by changing the tone. Think of yourself repeating an incident in the staff room. Do you use exactly the same tone as you used with the child? It is unlikely, because subconsciously, motivated as we are to maintain our own self-esteem, we tend to automatically choose the tone that validates our position. When I work with principals I encourage them to ask both teachers and students not just, "What was said?" but also, "How was it said?" The how is 90% of the story.

Is the purpose of punishment to hurt the child? It has elements of physical or emotional hurt: sarcasm or unreasonable penalties may be attached to it. The child does not learn to remedy the situation since punishment focuses on the problem rather than the solution. The punished child resents or fears the Punisher and will hide the truth. Punishment may be unexpected and the result of a capricious mood. If expected, it maybe too severe in the eyes of a child even though society might sanction it. Even a punished person has a choice, to comply or to be hurt. If a consequence is known in advance, they have some control. The true definition of punishment doesn't imply consequences are unknown. They may be known but may be too severe. It only takes one of these three aspects — too severe, unexpected, or subject to negative emotion — for a situation to be punishment to a child.

I met William Glasser when I worked in California for California Special Schools. Fred Miller Probation Camp was a forestry camp for young offenders aged fifteen to eighteen. In the morning the students had academic work. In the afternoon they worked with a forestry crew. I was a remedial therapeutic teacher — the only woman. I remember the first day I came to work. All across the camp reverberated the refrain, "All of a sudden I don't know how to read." As I worked with my reading groups I became aware of a strong phenomenon. My students preferred to interact with the forestry workers rather than with the camp counselors. I questioned them about this. They replied that although the forestry workers were almost paramilitary, having come from Germany, they were clear in their expectations, and the students always knew where they stood. On the other hand, the counselors tended to be 'go with the flow' people. They tended to be less clear about their expectations. When questioned, they would say to the boys who asked about furlough things like 'We'll see,' or 'We'll know when you're ready.' When asked about the decision-making process they would respond, 'We will decide when you're ready.' This kind of answer prevented the boys from feeling in control of their options. At worst, it was crazy making.

After this experience I decided the following.
I should:

- Be clear in my expectations.
- Be clear on consequences.
- State specifically what I needed to see
  in order to make a recommendation.
- Indicate at what level the decision would
  be made.

With the illusions of control in mind, let's take a closer look at the positions of control in relation to the dimensions of discipline vs. punishment.

The Punisher

Most of us learned about punishment from our experiences as children. When I went to school in the 1950's there was plenty of talk about punishment. Students were regularly subjected to punishment to bring them into line. Frequently, it was administered in public. I will never forget some of the faces of the boys in our school as they struggled to maintain composure after one, two, three, or more swats on the hand. Punishment hurt!

Some dictionary definitions of punishment are:

1. To subject (a person) to a penalty,
   such as imprisonment, a fine, or
   a beating for a crime, fault, offense,
   or misbehavior.
2. To handle roughly; injure; hurt.

Corporal punishment was the most obvious, for it left its mark. Sarcasm, humiliation, emotional abuse, and silence or isolation were others. Many teachers who applied these approaches believed that children were innately bad and would not behave unless they were forced or frightened into it. They had no concept of innate goodness. Alfie Kohn in an article 'Caring Kids' says,

> The belief persists in this culture that our darker side is more persuasive, more persistent, and somehow more real than our capacity for what psychologists call 'prosocial behavior.' We

seem to assume that people are naturally and primarily selfish and will act otherwise only if they are coerced into doing so and carefully monitored. The logical conclusion of this world view is the assumption that generous and responsible behavior must be forced down the throats of children who would otherwise be inclined to care only about themselves. *

His book, *The Brighter Side of Human Nature: Altruism and Empathy in Everyday Life,* refutes this prevailing point of view and stresses the nature of children's intrinsic goodness. He states in the article,

I believe that it is as 'natural' to help as it is to hurt, that concern for the well-being of others often cannot be reduced to self-interest, that social structures predicated on human selfishness have no claim to inevitability — or even prudence. **

Punishment is based on the idea that a child is basically self-centered and needs to be controlled. It is not effective in strengthening a child. What it can do is harden a child. A child who is frequently yelled at will no longer flinch. A child who is hit often will defiantly hold out his hand for more. Humiliation tends to train the child to rationalize pain and to repress normal feelings of hurt. Children also learn to hide in-

*Alfie Kohn, 'Caring Kids - The Role of the Schools', PhiDelta Kappan, March 1991, p. 498.
**Alfie Kohn - His article as above.

33

formation and to lie. Rather than be hurt, they often blame others for the problem. Punishment may be expedient for the teacher and gain short-term conformity. However its legacy is often long-lasting, anti-authority attitudes. There is a high probability that the Punisher's charges will grow up to be punitive to others if they are not exposed to another model.

I learned about punishment as a child. I grew up knowing that if I made a mistake something unpleasant would happen to me. Through this unpleasantness, I was told, I would learn not to make mistakes. Yet, try as I might, I was unable to eliminate mistakes. Some I chose, others just happened. Still others were out of my awareness. Regardless, the cycle was established: make a mistake, be caught, be corrected, feel bad, perhaps apologize, attempt to avoid the mistake, and, often, make the mistake again! Most of the mistakes I made as a child were not purposeful. They were the by-product of my attempting to get something from someone else, perhaps without enough thought for their needs and situation. Some of my transgressions were in retaliation for hurt done to me by peers or siblings. These tended not to be premeditated, but rather spur-of-the-moment actions of mine to offset their actions. Often I was asked to apologize; seldom was I asked to make a reparation. Always I felt like a bad person for a period of time.

I was a product of schooling in the 1950's. This was before the civil rights era of the 1960's. The adults of the 1950's believed it was their duty to impose their standards on children. Punishment was not relished by them, but they upheld their responsibilities. Most of us learned about punishment from our experiences as their children. We will use this same approach unless we consciously decide otherwise.

The Guilter

When adults are uncomfortable with the recognition of themselves as Punishers they may change their approach. They stop physical punishment and verbal abuse. They turn instead to moralizing and shaming. When did our species learn the art of shaming? Where did it all start? Can you visualize the way small children flush when they realize that we recognize their faults. This is the full moment of awareness that what they have done is unacceptable. It is a moment which each of us can vividly recall. Whether the shamer was parent or teacher, whether their intent was to raise guilt or to teach, the end result was the warm body flush that told us we were in the wrong. At that moment it seemed no absolution could reverse the tide of feeling.

One woman recalls stuttering as a second grade student when she tried to pronounce the sound of "s", so unfamiliar to her native tongue. The harder she tried, the worse she performed. She stood in front of her class eclipsed by shame. For myself, I can recall as a first grade student the horrible moment of wetting myself when the teacher held the class in after school and scolded us. I can remember shame when questioned by my neighbors as to why my father had not enlisted in World War II. Shame does not have to be justified to be experienced. Knowing one has blurted out a secret can bring a sense of guilt to a child, though his intent was innocent enough. There is an inherent bad feeling we experience when we don't meet our own expectations. We can bring guilt on ourselves by reviewing what we 'should' have done better. Some do it to the extent they are immobilized.

Somewhere along the line we humans learned to use this natural inclination of the individual to feel badly to control each other. We recognized that if the other person felt inadequate we were in a position to view ourselves as superior. We learned consciously to reflect back to the person their shortcomings in order to have the upper hand.

Again, power is the name of the game. Many teachers control the children in their classes through the use of guilt-inducing techniques. The more important the adult is to the child, the more effective is this approach. If the parents have told their child that a teacher is a person to be respected, the slightest disapproval from the teacher can be devastating for the child. He is not able to separate the teacher's opinion of him from who he really is. If the teacher says, 'I'm so disappointed in you,' the child takes the burden on his shoulders.

In his article, 'The Effect of School Failure on the Life of a Child,' William Glasser says that when a small child is asked what it means to have failed, the child usually replies, 'It means I'm a bad person.' When my daughter was in fourth grade she came home one day with broken glasses. She informed me it had been an accident on the playground. Several weeks later her sister learned she had been hit by her teacher when she was having difficulty with her math. When I asked her about it, my daughter confirmed the report. I asked her why she hadn't told me. She said, 'I thought you'd think I was a bad person.'

I searched my experience to understand how we had arrived at this point. I realized how often I had built up the teacher in her eyes. I had emphasized the authority of the teacher's role. I had told my children to get along with their teachers, so my daughter had assumed the fault was hers.

My attempt to transmit my values of respect for adults had been stronger than my teaching my child to respect herself. I had taught her to look outside herself for external moral valuation. I had not taught her to look inside herself and ask herself, 'Have I been a good person or a bad person?' I had inadvertently prepared her to be controlled by guilt. As teachers in schools, we intuitively recognize children who can be controlled in this manner. In our effort to maintain class control, we may lose sight of the repercussion of guilt on the child's self-esteem.

The Buddy

The Buddy is neither negative nor positive. It depends on the intent. Do we support the child to accomplish his goals or do we use the child's affection for us to accomplish our purposes? This is a complex issue. I believe in forming a positive relationship with the child. When I was a director of an alternate school I ran my whole program for a year and a half on my personal involvement with the students. For many of them I was the first adult who had shown genuine caring. I ran into difficulty, however, when I tried to reintegrate my students back into the mainstream. Although they would work for me, they would not work for other teachers. If I was called in to arbitrate, they would say, 'I will do it for you, Diane,' but their resolve was short-lived and dependent on my continued contact with them.

The Buddy position is not hurtful to the child, but it has little to do with discipline. When a person does something for us, he is not learning about society's limits nor is he learning about self-discipline. Once we have a friendship with a student I believe we are obligated to use it to help him evaluate his own behavior. We can get him to do this. He can't reject our questions, because we are in his internal world. If a teacher doesn't take this step, she is not fulfilling the potential of her relationship with the student. The Buddy position is an ideal springboard into restitution.

"Make a friend," says William Glasser in his book *Reality Therapy*. In *Schools Without Failure* he speaks even more strongly,

> Children who need affection desperately, not only from teachers but from each other, have little opportunity to gain that affection in school. To say that helping to fulfill the need for love is not a school function is tantamount to saying that children who don't succeed in giving and receiving desperately needed affection at home or in their community (outside of school) will have little chance to do so. Having failed to learn to love as a child, an adult is in a poor position ever to learn love. (Glasser, p. 13)

Being a friend to a child meets the child's need for connectedness. It also results in the child putting the teacher in his quality world so that he is receptive to the academic material and values we present. For children who are not getting the support they may need at home or the acceptance of their peers, the genuine interest of the teacher is crucial. Educational literature is full of stories about teachers who have made a difference in a child's life. For myself I can think of two students: one a teenage girl, the other a young offender in the correctional system, both of whom I consider friends to this day. Once a youngster establishes a strong bond of affection with the teacher, he will often attempt changes he would not address on his own. Generally speaking, this kind of relationship is positive; at its best, it is mutual.

There is one drawback to this relationship, which is the danger that the child will become too dependent on the adult. If the adult's opinion becomes more important to the child than their own self-evaluation then we are not helping the youth become a self-directed learner. This particular stage can be recognized by the student saying to the teacher, 'I'll do it for you,' and characteristically, that student will not grant to other adults the same respect he gives to the teacher he likes. He will behave for the Buddy, but no one else.

Another landmark of over-dependency is when the staff member tends to be too permissive with the student, making deals or letting him 'off the hook' when he misbehaves. The personal basis of the student's relationship to the school is a short-term benefit, but it is the responsibility of the teacher to begin to connect the student with other staff and students so that he can have connectedness with the whole program. Also, if the student is not so dependent on the teacher, conflicts can be more easily brought to the surface and resolved without the student rejecting the teacher and the school if disappointed.

In spite of the 'over dependent' drawback, the Buddy position is still of value. Show interest, use humor, and care about your students. But learn not to stop there. If a student says, 'I will do it for you,' say, "No, do it for yourself.'

The Monitor

Experienced teachers begin to recognize the effects of guilt on a child's self-esteem and seek other ways of influencing the child. Instead of criticizing or moralizing, we sometimes decide to devise a system wherein children can receive direct experiential feedback from their behavior. Instead of a teacher commenting on their behavior, we decide to use behavior modification techniques.

Most behavioral modification, stimulus-response programs have a system of positive reinforcement whereby children gain credits for being on task. These credits can be in the form of check marks, stars, marbles, etc. They generally represent a token economy and students can exchange them for concrete rewards (e.g. chocolate bars, games, or time off). This is a system of extrinsic rewards.

When I attended UCLA in 1967 I studied with Frank Hewitt, the founder of the Engineered Classroom. He built a very structured, operant conditioning program in which the teacher had a sterile, limited role. The teacher's job was to state calmly, every ten minutes, "You have been in your seat for ten minutes and have earned ten check marks," and to administer them. She would also say, "You have been on task for ten minutes and have earned ten check marks," and administer them. Personal involvement was discouraged. The student's relationship was between himself and his paper. If he didn't complete his work he received no check marks.

I did not pursue this course of studies, but I have through the years pondered at the short-term success of the students in this structured program. In retrospect, now that I have an understanding of internal motivation, I realize that the students had been put in a microcosm which helped them to understand the connection between what they did and what happened. Furthermore, by removing the human factor there was little chance for either positive or negative emotional control contributing to the interaction.

For a short time this offered the child a reprieve from commentary or control upon his actions. In the absence of external personal evaluation, he began to make self-evaluation of his actions based on the check marks he earned and what they could be traded for in concrete terms. I also noticed in this program that it worked best with primary children up to grade four, but seldom was it effective with any child after two years. The students just didn't want to be monitored any more. Their intrinsic need for freedom of choice rose to the fore.

Colleges of Education taught us to use positive reinforcement. It was one of the main tools taught to classroom teachers. Compliments, recognizing when children were on task, stars, stickers, marbles, and check marks were popular. We were also encouraged to remove such tokens for misbehavior. Assertive Discipline encourages the class to combine their rewards in order to have Friday parties. In Frank Hewett's program, check marks could be exchanged for chocolate bars or games.

I have experienced an incredible array of tantalizing reinforcements devised by teachers. Each of these works — for a while. The problem is that after a period of time the novelty wears off. The teacher then has to come up with a new, bigger, more exciting reward. This takes time and as I hear from teachers it is a considerable expense to them. In the structured programs, teachers report the reward system works well the first year. It is moderately effective the second year, if you vary the rewards. By the end of the second year, it is not working. This is the point at which I have been called in to consult in many programs.

The Monitor position of discipline has many positive features. The students appear to conform to positive strokes, rewards, and reasonable sanctions. They learn the expectations of the school. They learn what lines they can't cross. They learn that discomfort follows breaking the rules and they decide to avoid discomfort. The school runs smoothly. Students are calm, staff are satisfied. Schools which have used the stimulus-response version of the Reality Therapy vehicle for their journey are satisfied and may even become avid proponents of the approach. They may recommend to other schools their reward system, their time out approach, their sanctions. They believe that the child has been successfully educated in terms of his behavior.

Too many times, well-behaved students leave the system where they have conformed well for several years, and move into a situation where they have to make real-life choices and they have no tools. They may go wild because there are no clear limits to conform to, no immediate consequences or rewards, no one to monitor them. Most people can think of a family member or friend who moved away from home to school or to a job and then went wild for the first few months, sleeping in, staying up late, missing assignments, maybe drinking. For the students, it was a rough ride until they learned self-discipline.

Another example is a class which has run smoothly in a strict discipline model. When the children encounter a new teacher who wants to help them learn to make real choices, the children almost always take advantage of the new teacher. If the transition isn't carefully managed, they are "off the wall" because they don't know how to behave without strict limits and supervision.

I have always suggested to teachers who receive a class from a traditional teacher to set the rules for the class at first, telling them that after two weeks they will review the rules jointly to see if they are all needed. This way the children are gradually shifted to the democratic classroom.

The only choice many students have been making for years is the choice to avoid discomfort. When the teacher has asked, "Is it helping?", the students have hung their heads, shuffled, and answered, "No, M'am," in order to get off the hook. They have spent hours in detention, recopying work rather than investing in it, doing it only to avoid discomfort. They have apologized at least one hundred times by the time they leave elementary school. They have agreed to a variety of consequences and on some occasions have created their own penalties. The students are socialized into the system. They conform to expectations. They do what they are told. They avoid breaking the rules, but they still do not learn self- discipline.

Summary

Both punishing and guilting are punitive. Both monitoring and managing teach the child discipline. Monitoring teaches conformity to rules. Restitution as used by the Manager focuses on values to help the child learn self-discipline. The process will be punishment if it is any of the following: unexpected by the child, too severe, or uses hurting, emotional control. The process is discipline if it is expected, reasonable, and leads to an agreed upon consequence or to a restitution which strengthens the child.

Monitoring by teachers has produced students with the following traits: they behave to avoid discomfort; they wait to be rewarded externally for their efforts; they know how to 'do apologies,' 'do time,' and 'do penance.' If teachers want to make the transition from traditional discipline to restitution, they must help students learn how to accept their human frailties, to fix their mistakes, and to identify their needs.

Managing students, or the Manager, is the subject of the rest of this book.

"If you try to enforce duty only by the sword of state, you never create a moral being who has any interest in compliance or who feels obligated to do anything other than simply avoid the penalties of law."

— *Benjamin Barber*

Chapter Three

Restitution

Restitution is the action of repairing a damage done. *If we break it, we cry; If you break it, you buy* reads the sign in a glassware department. What principle lies herein? Can you recall parental messages such as, 'If you mess it up, you clean it up,' or 'If you break it, you fix it'? What does the New Testament say about restitution? What do the folk tales tell us about restitution? What is restitution?

Sometimes it is in the form of financial repayment. Restitution can be in the form of repayment of time. Often it is in the form of labor given in return for a misdemeanor or public reinstatement of "face." A creative restitution takes into consideration not only the negative act, but also the effect the act has had on the victim. The result should be that the victim is compensated or reinstated. Restitution is discipline, not punishment.

Punishment often leaves both the offender and the victim injured or feeling like failures. An 'eye for an eye' does not bring better vision for anyone. A 'tooth for a tooth' tends to leave the offender with few resources to make restitution. Punishment impresses that a person has done wrong but tends to leave the person feeling guilty or angry. It does not empower him to address the wrong and to deliver what the victim would consider adequate compensation.

Restitution sounds like a perfectly good principle. Do you believe in it? More important, do you practice it? What do you do when you are having a party and one of your friends breaks a glass? Would you let her pay to have it replaced? If you have taken a taxi to a meeting only to find the person who asked for the meeting has forgotten the appointment and is otherwise engaged, would you let that person pay for your taxi fare? If an employee has made a costly error and offers to repay it by overtime work without salary, would you accept his offer?

At one time I would have refused to accept any of these offers of reimbursement. I would have answered these inquiries with comments such as, 'Never mind,' 'It doesn't matter,' 'No problem,' 'Forget it!' I would have been gracious, because that is was how I was raised.

What would you do? If someone who has wronged you in the past asks to make amends, would you allow them to do so? If a child spills his milk, would you let him clean it up? If a colleague has forgotten to do a piece of work, would you say, 'Never mind, I've done it for you'? If a person you are expecting to give you a ride keeps you waiting, would you accept his offer to help you with your errands? What did your family teach you about restitution?

What do you do when a child makes a mistake?
- Do you draw it to his attention?
- Do you tell him he should have known better?
- Do you remind him of similar failures?
- Do you ask him why he did what he should not have done?
- Do you criticize him or give the silent treatment?

I know what I used to do.
- I drew it to his attention.
- I told him he should know better.
- I reminded him of similar failures.
- I asked him why he did what he should not have done.
- I criticized him or gave him the silent treatment.

This approach resulted in my feeling omnipotent. The child felt like a failure.

Restitution is an idea whose time has come, but I do not believe it has been a prevailing ethic of our culture to date. Our old habits will be hard to break. The accepted practice when someone has wronged us has been either to say 'never mind' or, more likely, to cause them discomfort in some manner, to seek retribution. We have been intent on focusing on their wrong-doing rather than searching together for a way for them to make amends. We've been more concerned with them paying the price in discomfort than regaining self-esteem through righting a wrong. 'Getting even' has been more important than 'making it right.'

Mistakes happen; accidents are a part of life. Restitution is about making things right. Restitution is the opportunity for an individual who has made a mistake to make full reparation to the best of his ability at the present or in the near future. Restitution enables the individual to reclaim self-esteem through personal effort. Restitution benefits the person wronged; it also benefits the person who has done the wrong.

'IT IS OKAY TO MAKE A MISTAKE.
NOW WHAT ARE YOU GOING TO DO TO FIX IT?'
Forgiveness is not the same as restitution. Forgiveness is bestowed by the victim. It can offer relief to the wronged party but it does not set the stage for the repair of self-esteem by an act of compensation.

'IT IS ALRIGHT TO SAY YOU'RE SORRY.
NOW WHAT ARE YOU GOING TO DO TO FIX IT?'
In our culture we tend to focus on consequences to actions. We attempt not to interfere with natural consequences. We are prone to create logical consequences. The consequence could be to make a restitution for the harmful act, but most frequently the consequence tends to be set as a loss of privilege or a restriction of freedom. With children we tend to ground them at home or give them detention at school; we hold them back from activities they enjoy. Each of these approaches is designed to make the child uncomfortable and falls in the category of monitoring. None of these approaches strengthens the child. None allows him the opportunity to make a reparation to the person wronged. Each exacts a price.

If we continuously focus on reparation rather than on fault we will become proactive rather than reactive. The act of restitution is a healing act for the person who has done wrong, and it has the potential to remedy the wrong for the victim. Moreover, the person who effects the restitution will be stronger than they were before they erred. This is the real power of the process. The person who has erred does not return to a neutral state. He is actually positively impacted by his act of restitution. He is a better person. People cannot change what has been done. People cannot change the past. People can only change what they do next.

You are one person. The child you guide is another. What will you do next? What can he or she do next to make it right? The next time someone wrongs you, will you let them right their wrong? Will you let your guest replace the glass? What could be the benefit to her? Would it hurt you? Could it benefit you? As for the taxi fare, would you accept a compensation? What could be the benefit to him? Would it hurt you? Will you allow your employees to pay back what they lose? What could be the benefit to them? to you? And so it goes — with the spilled milk, the forgotten task, and the late ride. Would it benefit each of these individuals to make it right? Would it benefit you to aid them to make it right? Would you gain from their making it right or do you want to say, "Never mind"?

How I Learned Restitution

I learned the concept of restitution as I applied the ideas of Reality Therapy with my three children. As a young mother the manner in which I disciplined my children was very much as I had been disciplined. I scolded, gave consequences, removed privileges, and sent them to their rooms. I collected an enormous number of dimes, quarters, and dollars as fines for misbehavior, and my girls spent a lot of time grounded for breaking the rules.

It was not until I raised my third child, Jacob, that I really understood that good discipline didn't need to cause pain. Through an understanding of Control Theory* I began to realize that any time there was a frustration in the system there was a negative expenditure of energy. The planning phase was robbed as the child struggled with guilt or anger. I began to try to give up a negative focus. Rather than commenting on the offense, I made the assumption that my child was willing to make restitution. "What's your plan to fix it?" became my key question in discipline situations. I also began to utilize more phrases such as:

It's okay to make a mistake.
You're not the only one.
I know you didn't mean for it to turn out this way.
I'm not interested in your mistake — I'm interested in what you're going to do about it.

Reality Therapy and *Control Theory* - William Glasser, MD.

Having said these things, we then began to look for ways for him to make amends. My job, I discovered, was to frame up the direction of the solution. I learned to do this from William Powers's example of the birds' nesting concept. He says a bird cannot have too specific a concept of a nest or it will not be flexible enough to survive. For example, if a bird only had a picture of a twig nest then it could not survive if it found itself above the treeline. Rather, the brain gives us a fuzzy general picture which we can make more specific depending on the resources in the environment.

Understanding this concept, I began to set a general direction and give parameters to my son rather than generating specific solutions. I heard myself say things like,

> *It has to take time and effort on your part.*
> *She has to be satisfied with the result.*
> *It should be in the same general area as the offense.*
> *It needs to be a genuine amend.*
> *It can't be too easy.*
> *It should help you get stronger.*

I would like to stress that even now, when my son and I understand restitution, we don't always use it. Sometimes when I am angry, I lay guilt on him by recalling past failures. Sometimes if I am frustrated or lack time to work things out, I just assign a consequence. More and more often, however, I find that Jacob comes to me with the report of a misdemeanor and a proposed solution. With my third child, focusing on restitution has made a big difference. He only stays in his room until he figures out how to remedy a misbehavior, and he never loses an allowance. It is the direction in which we are going that is important. He is becoming stronger and more independent. I have taught him the values I believe are important. Now, he has to decide what his values are. Next year he will be sixteen, which some consider to be the age of manhood. I hope that by using the process of restitution Jacob will be the kind of man who is an employee who fixes his mistakes, a father who helps his child learn a better way, a manager who leads rather than bosses those he supervises.

The Characteristics of Restitution

A good restitution will have the following characteristics:

- It will be seen by the victim as adequate compensation.
- It will require effort on the part of the offender.
- It does not in any way encourage further offenses.

An exceptional restitution will have three other characteristics:

- It will be relevant to the general area of the offense.
- It will be tied to a higher value or mission statement so the child doesn't see the restitution as an isolated event, but part of a larger picture of how people treat each other.
- It strengthens the child.

Successful restitution is also characterized by the lack of certain negative behaviors in the adult:

- Restraint of criticism, guilt, anger.
- Lack of feeling in the helping adult of resentment or being overextended.

If the adult uses criticism, guilt, or anger the child is unlikely to participate willingly in restitution. If the adult feels overextended or resentful, he or she is doing more work than the offender.

It is not essential that the restitution meet all the requirements, but these guidelines are something to work toward, and both you and the children you work with will become more creative in your solutions.

An Example of "Making It Right"

One day my son Jake came home from school and recounted an argument he'd had with Anthony that morning. As he told the story, one of the words he used was racist. I stopped him and pointed this out. His response was 'I didn't know.' I went on, 'I understand that you didn't know any better, but in our family we don't use words like that.' This was the family mission statement about our stand on racism.

Then I asked Jake to make restitution. I said, "You need to set this right with Anthony, or people will think we believe words like that are okay." Jake responded that Anthony had called him a name, one questioning his sexual orientation. I explained that Anthony's prejudices were the responsibility of his family; Jake's responsibility was to correct the image of our family. I suggested he go to his room and figure out what to do.

Twenty minutes later I heard Jake make a phone call from the other room. His end of the conversation went like this, 'Anthony, I meant everything I said except _____, and my mom says if I say that, you'll think we're racist and we're not. Bye.'

This simple example illustrates several of the important points about restitution.

- The restitution was an attempt to redress a wrong.
- The restitution was within the framework of a family or societal value.
- The restitution was accomplished by the wrong-doer finding his own solution to appease the victim.
- The restitution was not preceded by criticism or moralizing about the crime or the punishment.
- The emphasis was on compensation and learning a better way.

Often I have found that it works best if I frame up the direction of the solution. If a wall is dirtied, the restitution of cleaning it is easily chosen. Sometimes, however, a redress of the grievance is not obvious, in which case the person needs a general direction in which to look to develop a solution. Many times the restitution needs to be negotiated. Sometimes this involves the victim.

In this example the compensation may not have healed the wound, but it was in the right general direction. It required effort. It indicated the offense would not be repeated. It was a verbal retraction for a verbal affront. It was tied to a higher family value.

Another Example: Snowballs

In Saskatchewan, where we have a lot of snow in the winter, I live in a flat-roofed house. One day I had hired my twelve-year-old son and his friend to shovel the roof for $10.00. I sat in my living room listening to them energetically running back and forth above my head intent on their task — or so I thought. Suddenly there was a knock at my door, and a very angry man informed me that two kids on my roof were throwing ice balls. Suddenly I had a different picture of the energy being expended so enthusiastically above.

I was upset! I struggled for control. I called the boys down from the roof. I said to them, 'This is not what I want to be hearing when I open my door, that two boys are throwing ice snowballs at cars. What you did could have hurt people. We don't do that in this family.'

They were chagrined. I struggled to move away from my anger toward restitution. It was difficult. They could not undo what they had done. The man from the street had left. What needed to happen?

I haltingly framed my request, 'Alright, boys. Sam, you go home. Jake, you go to your room. Figure out what you can do to make this right. What you did could have hurt people, so you need to figure out something to do to help people — and it has to have something to do with ice and snow.'

They responded, 'Just don't give us the $10.00.' I said, 'No, that's not good enough. The issue here is not the money, the issue is throwing icy snowballs that could have caused an accident or a broken windshield. You need to figure out how to make amends.'

They stared at me uncomprehending. I was not at all that sure that I could get a restitution here, but because the offense was so serious I wanted to try for it. I repeated myself and added firmly, 'I have confidence you can work this out. Talk to each other on the phone, then let me know what you decide. If you need my input, come and ask.'

Sam scooted out the door. The moment he was gone, what do you think Jake said? You guessed it. 'Sam did it, not me.' I gave my standard response to such shifting of the blame. 'You were there, so you share responsibility.' Jake swore, something he rarely does, certainly not at his parents. I resisted the temptation to shove him and stayed in control. I said, 'And figure out what you're going to do about that too!' I turned and walked away into the living room, collapsed on the couch, and wondered if this could be worked out. Jake went to his room. Over the next hour and a half there were a series of phone calls back and forth. Finally, Sam arrived at the door with a bag of ice salt and I relaxed knowing the solution was in progress.

This was the plan. The boys had made some phone calls. They would go over to Jake's sixty-year-old baby-sitter and clean her walk and put ice salt on it. Then they would go to Sam's grandpa's home in the trailer court to clean the ice off his windows so he could get out if there were a fire. I had reservations about the efficiency of the second plan, but I kept my mouth shut because they were invested in it and it was in the general direction I had requested.

I accepted this plan of restitution. The boys then said "You need to drive us." I quickly thought about it. Am I willing to spend my Saturday afternoon this way? Can I do it without resentment? Whose job is this? I replied, "This is not my restitution! You need to find your own way over there. Here's the number of the transit system for the schedule. I'll give you the bus fare." After another half-hour of planning they were on their way.

Three hours later they returned triumphant, their pockets full of cookies. There were stories of how they figured out their jobs. There was the incident of Sam cutting his hand on the sharp ice. (Dreikurs would call this "natural consequences," I called it "poetic justice" and had a hard time not commenting thusly.) There was the gratefulness of the elders and the pride of the boys in negotiating the bus transfers. They had learned, they were strengthened, and the odds were they would think twice about throwing ice snowballs again.

After Sam left, Jake came over to me with a fist full of change. He said "This is $1.69, all the money I have in the world, and I think I should give this to you for swearing at you." My brain began to rev up for restitution, but I was tired, he was tired and I couldn't think of how to frame up a restitution. I said, 'OK, I'll take your money.' He heaved a sigh of relief saying, 'Oh, thank you.' Giving me a hug, he wearily retired.

I learned a lot working out this restitution with the boys. It was the first time I had gone for something this big, and this unclearly defined. Also, I was not used to involving another person's child in our restitutions. That day I learned to have confidence: confidence in the process, confidence in myself as a parent trying to work it out, and confidence in the boys' ability to create a beneficial solution.

Analyzing a Restitution

In the snowball example, which of the characteristics of restitution do you think were present?

1. Satisfactory amends to the victim.
   No, remedy was made to a surrogate.

2. Effort required from offender.
   Yes, the plan for transportation, getting the salt to melt the ice, doing the work, paying the money.

3. Little incentive for repetition of the offense.
   Yes, they realize ice was hard and could hurt.

4. Relevant to the 'crime' where possible.
   Yes, involved ice, snow, and helping.

5. Tied to a higher value, mission statement.
   Yes, we don't have fun in ways that hurt people.

6. Strengthens the person who has offended.
   Yes, they learned how to make it right.

7. No resentment by the planner/helper.
   Yes, I didn't overextend myself.

8. Restraint of criticism, guilt, or anger.
   Yes/No, I think I had anger in my voice at the beginning, but I didn't use guilt.

Examples for You to Analyze

Learning to Sew

Two fourth grade boys scuffled on the playground. Evert grabbed Thomas and ripped three buttons off his shirt. The playground supervisor sent them in to speak to the principal. The principal reminded Evert about the school belief in respect for each other. She asked Evert if he would be willing to make up to Thomas for what he had done. He nodded. She then asked Thomas what he wanted. Thomas said 'I need my buttons fixed. My mom's going to kill me!" The principal asked Evert if he'd be willing to sew Thomas's buttons back on. Outraged, Evert retorted, 'I don't know how to sew!' She asked him if he would be willing to learn to sew. He answered, "Who will teach me?" She said, "The teaching assistant." Evert agreed and spent the noon hour learning to sew and repairing Thomas's shirt. Last seen, Thomas was arm-in-arm with Evert on the playground.

In the 'Learning to Sew' example, which of the characteristics of restitution do you think were present?

_____ 1. Satisfactory amend to the victim.

_____ 2. Effort required from offender.

_____ 3. Little incentive for repetition of the offense.

_____ 4. Relevant to the 'crime' where possible.

_____ 5. Tied to a higher value, mission statement.

_____ 6. Strengthens the person who has offended.

_____ 7. No resentment by the planner/helper.

_____ 8. Restraint of criticism, guilt, or anger.

A Better Way to Treat You

A class of middle school students acted rudely to a substitute teacher. They talked continuously while she was attempting to teach the class, and when she tried to address them, they laughed. Three girls were targeted as the culprits. When their teacher returned to school, she confronted them with the note from the substitute teacher and asked them what they could do to make restitution. The girls debated a bit, then offered to apologize. The teacher said they could do so if they wished, then asked them what they could do to make restitution. They had a discussion with the teacher about how they should treat people in their classroom. They made the evaluation that their behavior was not in line with the school's beliefs. The girls proposed that they could initiate a discussion with the rest of their classmates about how they should behave next time. Then they would write a letter to the substitute teacher informing her of their decision. They would also tell her they were writing a letter to the principal to request her as a substitute the next time their teacher was away in order to behave a better way next time.

In the 'A Better Way to Treat You' example, which of the characteristics of restitution do you think were present?

_____ 1. Satisfactory amend to the victim.

_____ 2. Effort required from offender.

_____ 3. Little incentive for repetition of the offense.

_____ 4. Relevant to the 'crime' where possible.

_____ 5. Tied to a higher value, mission statement.

_____ 6. Strengthens the person who has offended.

_____ 7. No resentment by the planner/helper.

_____ 8. Restraint of criticism, guilt, or anger.

The Air Pump

This is a story about what can happen when we make restitution hard to accomplish.

A young boy on vacation in Mexico broke his Grandpa's air pump when he was attempting to pump up his raft. Upset, he came to his mother. 'I don't know what to do,' he said. 'I've tried to fix this and I don't think there are any of these down here to buy.' She said 'It's okay to make a mistake,' and softly suggested that he approach Grandpa, explain the situation, and ask how he could repay him for the mistake.

Then Grandma arrived on the scene. She was of the old school who believed it is essential that children know when they've made a mistake. She said, 'Look what you've done! You've broken our air pump! You should have known better. We can't get another one here.' The boy's mother attempted to explain that he knew he'd made a mistake, he just didn't know how to make an amend for it. Meanwhile the boy disappeared. The debate on child disciplining practices continued.

A while later the child returned and whispered in his mom's ear. 'I was feeling bad so I went downstairs and had a little cry.' His mom nodded in sympathy, then said, 'Now, what can you do to sort this out with Grandpa?' The boy's face hardened. He was no longer willing to make restitution since he felt he had taken his punishment through scolding and guilt.

What Do You Do When ...?

1. A student calls someone a name

Punish	Monitor	Restitution
Humiliate in front of class	Name on the board. Loss of privilege	Tell the other person some-thing nice

2. Students are throwing rocks at the bus stop

Punish	Monitor	Restitution
Yell at them and point	Kick the kids off the bus	Have them clean up the bus stop and figure out what positive ac-tivity they can do tomorrow while waiting

3. A student is writing on the wall

Punish	Monitor	Restitution
Slap his hand	Have him write 100 sen-tences 'I will not deface school prop-erty.'	Have him clean wall during re-cess and start a scrapbook for doodling

4. A child is caught stealing

Punish	Monitor	Restitution
Yell, humiliate in front of peers	Detention	Child decides to give it back and asks the victim what he can do to make amends

5. Children are hitting or punching in line up

Punish	Monitor	Restitution
Send to principal for a strap	Time out on bench; Send to the end of line	Make plan to do better

6. Absenteeism

Punish	Monitor	Restitution
Suspension	Detention	If you missed time we need you to make up the work. What's your plan?

7. Talks on the story rug

Punish	Monitor	Restitution
Yell at him	Send him to his seat	Choose something for him to do for classroom

The principle of restitution can be applied from the simplest to the most complex situations. The following are missed opportunities for restitution. What would be a better way to handle each of these situations? What approach would strengthen the person who made the mistake?

1. A child spills his milk and hastily says, 'I'll clean it up.' The mother says, 'Never mind I'll do it,' and pushes the child away, doing his task for him.

2. An employer asks an employee for a report. It isn't finished but the employee says, 'I'll finish it at noon hour.' The boss says, 'Never mind, I'll do it' and removes the incomplete report from the employee's hand.

3. A wife asks her husband if he phoned the maintenance man. He says, 'No, I'll do it right now.' She says, 'Never mind, I already did it.'

4. A teenager used some of his parents money without permission. He feels guilty, confessess, and wants to pay them back. They say, 'Never mind, we just won't trust you again.'

Summary

A restitution is characterized by the following:

- Tied to a higher value, mission statement.

- Strengthens the person who has offended.

- Satisfactory amend to the victim.

- Effort required from offender.

- Relevant to the 'crime' where possible.

- Little incentive for repetition of the offense.

- No resentment by the planner/helper.

- Restraint of criticism, guilt, or anger.

One can achieve a restitution with the student by:

- Talking about the value to be protected — what we believe.

- Asking the child if he cares about being part of the group or telling him you want him to be part of the group.

- Framing the restitution to include both the child's needs and the needs of the teacher or group.

- Allowing the student time to create a personal solution.

Restitution Options:

- Fix

- Payback

- Say two positives about person

- Give time in lieu

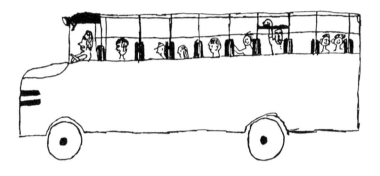

"At every step the child should be allowed to meet the real experiences of life; the thorns should never be plucked from the roses."

— *Ellen Key*

Chapter Four

Moving Toward Self-Discipline

Building a less coercive environment in the classroom, where self-discipline and restitution can occur, requires a progression of student management techniques.

Step One

Opening Up the Territory

The first step of the process is to reduce the number of interventions. As we have discussed, adults who use traditional discipline practices tend to monitor children closely, giving them considerable feedback and positive reinforcement. Anyone's attempt to stop a person from doing what he or she is doing will create frustration. The child will tend to resist any change we suggest. This resistance will necessitate an investment of energy from us. I advise both parents and teachers to ask themselves, before they attempt an intervention, 'Does it really matter?'

As teachers, we need to assess the amount of energy necessary to attain change and decide if what we want is worth this effort. Such assessment will help us begin to reduce the number of our interventions with children, thus "opening up the territory." By doing this we can ensure that our to interventions are likely to be noticed, because the child will not be habituated to our monitoring. Opening up the territory with the child will give the child more freedom. Freedom is necessary for the child to develop responsibility through making choices. No child can learn responsibility without exploring options and learning from his decisions. Space between the adult and the child is essential. Most teachers initially resist this suggestion, but when they experiment with it they report less conflict with the child as well as more freedom from responsibility for themselves. Opening up the territory is not a laissez-faire, permissive approach. Rather, the teacher decides what he or she believes is really important to monitor in terms of goals in the classroom, and then focuses on these principles.

Hold Fast to Your Values
and Let the Rest Go

There are three exercises that deal with the concept of shifting from a negative to a positive focus: "Does It Really Matter?," "Yes, If," and "Complain to Me." As teachers engage in these activities they understand at a visceral level the difference between addressing a child on the failure or the success side.

Does it Really Matter?

When we adults find ourselves monitoring and controlling children, we can ask ourselves, 'Does it really matter?' Is it necessary for their safety or to protect what we believe in? We should never set a limit or a condition unless we can explain to the child why it is important. 'Do it because I said!' is not an adequate answer. The child must be given a reasonable explanation. The more areas of the child's life we can give up controlling, the more the child will listen to us when it is really important. Over-controlling a child's behavior may result in blind obedience, in which case the child doesn't develop self-discipline or the ability to use probability determination to make good choices. The other result of over-monitoring is that the child may begin to tune us out so he doesn't hear us when the request is very important for safety.

There are certain areas where we do decide it is important to limit a child. Think about the following examples from a classroom teacher's perspective. These examples are dependent on circumstances and age. There may be a wide diversity in the answers given, and usually there is a qualifying condition necessary.

Does It Really Matter?

If he sits with his feet on the floor?
If she chews gum or not?
If they are silent while working?
If she pays attention?
If he does his homework?
If she fails an exam?
If they want to change seats?
If he joins an extracurricular activity?
If she writes neatly?
If he understands the lesson?
If she participates in a class discussion?
If he reads books?
If he wears an earring?
If he shows up on time?
If she has a clean desk?
If he hands in an assignment late?
If she puts her hand up before talking?

If you have answered 'Yes' to any of the above, what reason would you give the child why you are requiring compliance?

Yes, If ...

This activity requires teachers to identify requests from students to which they have been responding with the answer 'No' or 'No, because.' Such requests are simple ones such as 'Can I sharpen my pencil?' The answer has been 'No, because I'm talking.' A better answer would be one which redirects the child such as 'Yes, when I'm finished giving instructions.'

The general idea is to increase the number of positive responses you give to student requests. To do this:

1. Say 'Yes' as often as you can.

2. If you can't say 'Yes,' say 'Yes if ...' and add the condition necessary to be able to say yes to the person.

3. When you say 'No,' give the child your reason and don't change your mind.

Teachers have a lot of fun doing this activity first in small groups of four or five. Then they chose an example to share with the group. When this happens, we who have worked in the classroom recognize ourselves and do a lot of laughing and learning.

(Activity from *The Identity Society,* William Glasser, MD.)

Examples

May I sharpen my pencil?

- No, you should've done that before class.
- Yes, if there is no one else at the sharpener and I am not talking.

May we listen to the radio?

- No, because it would be too distracting.
- Yes, if everyone is on task.

May I go to the bathroom?

- No, because then everyone will want to go.
- Yes, if you wait until I've finished my instruction and only one person goes at a time.

May we go to Sea World?

- No, it's too expensive and we have no chaperones.
- Yes, if you can raise the money, get chaperones and do the study in advance.

May we have a dance?

- No, because I said.
- Yes, if we can have a month to plan it.

Complain to Me!

This exercise introduces the concept of switching a negative complaint into a positive want. It is a role play with two people — one the complainer and one the complaint receiver. The idea is to practice the appropriate questions that turn the complaint from a 'don't want' to a 'do want' and then to a solution to the problem.

1. How do you want it to be? *(Instead of how you don't want it to be.)* Can you control this?

2. What have you been doing to get what you want?

3. Is it working?

4. Do you want to figure out a better way?

- If the answer is 'No,' then ask, 'Do you just want to complain?' Then let the person complain vigorously for two minutes.

- If the answer is 'Yes,' then make a plan.

Step Two

Gaining Consent: The Social Contract

Once the territory is opened up we need to begin to work on the concept of consent. Each of us is an individual with free will. In order to share a common goal we must want to be part of a group. If a child decides it is more satisfying to be part of a group than to be alone an adult can ask the child to subscribe to certain principles that the group decides are important in order to co-exist. In the classroom there are three areas that can be negotiated to get agreement:

- The agreement between the teacher and the students as to each of their roles in the class.
- What we as a group believe in — our values.
- The rules we will choose to support what we value.

Decisions of this nature can resolve the conflict a person can feel between his individual freedom and his desire to meet his belonging need with the group. Discussions of these three issues increase involvement between the adult and children. It lifts the burden of responsibility for class behavior from being solely on the teacher, so she has more freedom. Also, both the adult and the students can feel a sense of increased control as together they have established guidelines and limits. In our society we have emphasized individual rights but seem to have lost our understanding of obligations to the group that accompany the rights we gain from being part of that group. There are duties which accompany membership in any relationship. Children gain personal power and are enriched by the opportunity to serve the group. As one author puts it, "America's youth has learned only half of the democratic equation: They have almost no sense of civic participation and responsibility." *

Once an individual has entered into a social contract as a member of the group, the individual gives up some personal freedom in return for the benefits of membership. The individual decides consciously or unconsciously to allow the group to control him. This control may be implemented by the group as peer pressure. More often it is exerted by a recognized representative of the group. In the classroom this person is usually the teacher. If a child decides he wants to be part of the class, he is accepting certain conditions. The least of these must be the obligation to manage himself in a manner that does not interfere with others meeting their needs.

There is debate whether a child should be forced to do school work in class. Personally, I feel such coercion would interfere with his choosing learning for his own benefit. I support the right of a child to withhold consent to learn during class if he sits quietly and does not interfere with others learning. It is also important not to rescue the child by persuading him to learn or by

*Mary Ann Glendor, Harpers Magazine, February 1991.

interfering with natural consequences when he has nothing completed for evaluation. My experience has been that few children will sit for more than two days without re-engaging themselves in the learning process if the classroom has something worth learning and the teacher is actively engaged with the rest of the class. At this point, the child becomes a self-directed learner.

If the child disturbs others who want to learn, the teacher has the right to use the agreed upon rules of the class to remove him. However, it would not be the first choice. Usually, when it gets to the point that removal is necessary, it is because the child has become aggravated by attempts to coerce him to work. If we offer our help and then allow him to sit, his disruptive behavior is less likely to escalate.

Step Three

Setting and Maintaining Limits

If the child hurts others, the teacher has the right to use control on him. The social contract gives her this right to keep the class a safe place to be.

Once the child understands that his choices will be respected and that he has an obligation to the group, he is in a position to teach himself. How he does this is through turning his mistakes into learning opportunities. Every answer not known is a learning to be embraced. Every rude remark given is a chance to make an amend to a member of the group. Anything broken is an opportunity for a repair. Learning a better way through creating a new behavior gives innate pleasure.

The exercises that deal with discipline are "My Job Is" and "What's the Rule?"

My Job Is

This exercise sets out the role of the teacher and the student. Developed jointly between the teacher and the students, it gives direction. It also specifies examples of jobs that are not legitimate expectations of the teachers or the students. This gives the students the concept of the limitations and roles of both the teacher and themselves.

This exercise displays clearly where the power lies and shows how the authority is commensurate with the responsibility.

MY JOB IS to ...	YOUR JOB IS to ...
teach	learn
answer questions	ask if you don't understand
explain different ways	keep on trying
be there on time	tell me if I go to fast
go at pace you can learn	follow the rules
do class management	communicate your needs
enforce rules	listen to me and others
care	

MY JOB IS NOT ...	YOUR JOB IS NOT ...
to take abuse	to do my job
to babysit; taxi	to decide for another child
to lend money	to discipline others
to do your job	
to cover up	

Role Involvement Phrases

When we are working with kids, we are involved with them in two ways: the first is personal involvement, the second is role involvement. Role involvement describes the power relationship, regardless of the nature of the personal relationship. Role involvement phrases are useful when your personal involvement with a student interferes with the job to be done.

- The rule is ...

- The policy is ...

- What we decided ...

- I'm in a position ...

- From my experience ...

What's the Rule?

The exercise "What's the Rule?" shows teachers how to focus on the expectations established collaboratively with the class. This exercise can achieve the following:

- A way to save time.
- The importance of not talking too much at the moment of discipline.
- How to emphasize the solution rather than the problem.
- How to use the pause and thank you.
- How to avoid debate and excuses.

1. Ask "What's the rule?"
   If the child doesn't know or won't say it, repeat the rule yourself.
2. Ask "Can you do that?"
   Don't require a verbal answer, a nod is adequate.
3. Say "Thank you, I appreciate it."

By using this method you will avoid many confrontations. If the rule is stated in the negative, this method won't be effective because in stating the rule for you the child will feel guilty. If the rule is repeated in the positive, the child remains on the success side. Thus he is more likely to cooperate and less likely to act out or withdraw. A strong suggestion here is to avoid moralizing, lecturing, or pointing out his breaking of the rule. He knows what he did. He made a social contract with the class. The question is, can he change his behavior?

Rules for Rules

William Glasser gives the following guidelines for rule making.

- A rule needs to be stated in the positive.
- There should be few rules. Children can't remember too many.
- A rule must be enforceable. Otherwise drop it.
- Be willing to change a rule if it doesn't work.
- Children need to know the rules and have helped to make them.
- When a rule is broken something must happen.

Maintaining Limits

Once the rules are set try to maximize positive interactions between yourself, as teacher, and your students. To do this spell out clearly the following:

This is How You Get What You Want From Me	This Doesn't Work On Me
• Word it as a question.	• Crying
• Ask me.	• Whining
• Raise your hand.	• Arguing
• Speak clearly.	• Saying, "Everyone is
• Be pleasant.	doing it."
• Use logic.	
• Tell me what you need.	

Time Out

From my experience, schools use time out too frequently in a punitive manner. Time out will not work unless students use it to improve themselves. If we use either a punitive or guilt-instilling tone, the time out will be perceived as punitive. Then the students will focus on giving us what we want rather than focusing on becoming the person they want to be.

There are other problems with time out. One is that the time out can be more need-fulfilling than the classroom. This happens when several misbehaving students are together in time out and they can interact, topping each other with their exploits, having fun and freedom from the class routine.

If students are given a lot of positive involvement from the staff person supervising time out, they may begin to like being sent out because they have a buddy with whom to talk. This can also happen when misbehaving students are sent to a kindly principal or vice principal who does not require enough change from them.

Another problem may be that the child becomes bored with plan making. He writes his plan as fast as he can, just to get out of time out. This usually happens when teachers do not have time to follow up on the plan, so the plan becomes meaningless. At worst it can become a joke among students who just say, 'Give me an action plan.'

The solution in this case is to move the plan concept toward restitution. It is not enough for a student to write, 'I won't do it again.' In-depth planning is needed to focus on restitution rather than elimination of the problem behavior.

Worksheet for Student

The following is a sample worksheet that can be filled in by a misbehaving student during time out to guide him in making a plan for restitution.

1. What I did.

2. How I was meeting my needs.

3. Do I have the right to meet my own needs?

4. How I interfered with (name)_____meeting their need for _____. (Love, power, fun, freedom, safety).

5. Do I care about (name)_____'s need for _____? (Go talk with a helper about this.)

6. What will I do?

7. Do I want help? What help?

8. How will we know this plan is working?

9. When will it be done?

10. How will this plan help me?

Summary

- Opening Up the Territory

Teachers need to ask "Does it really matter?" before they intervene with a child's behavior. We can also practice saying "Yes, if" more often than "No, because" because this answer directs children to problem solve. We should practice asking "What do we need to figure out?" because it focuses toward the solution rather than asking "What's the problem?" which leads to complaining.

- Gaining Consent: The Social Contract

Teachers can use several procedures to build with their students a common picture of how they will work together in the classroom. The first part of this process is the discussion with the children about the ideal classroom picture and the values they want to hold as a group. These are always related back to the district and school mission statements. The second part of the picture is built by negotiating roles, rules, and consequences.

- Setting and Maintaining Limits

Setting limits revolves around the students doing their job and the teacher doing her job which is to help them to do their job.

"Childhood is
the most basic human right
of children."

— David Elkind

Chapter Five

Managing Difficult Situations

With mainstreaming, teachers are having to become more effective managers of difficult students. Ideally restitution would be practiced with all students, all the time. It is our goal, but we work slowly toward it.

One high school staff told me that six months after being introduced to restitution they believed they were using it 90% of the time. This then is a reasonable goal with high school students. However, not all elementary school students are ready for restitution. Some little ones have not made the connection between what they do and what happens. They may first need some monitoring in the form of clear consequences. Other students being mainstreamed for the first time don't want to work without positive reinforcement in terms of stickers and prizes. The student who answers 'I don't know' is one of the most difficult children to work with. Patient use of the questions of Reality Therapy in a non-coercive manner can help the person make decisions. This chapter focuses on the questions of Reality Therapy as a vehicle for less coercive management of difficult children.

Reality Therapy is a positive, action-oriented approach to help people take more effective control of their lives. It teaches people to identify what they want, what they need, and what they are currently doing to get it. This approach asks the individual to evaluate his current behavior and to make decisions to change, or in some cases not to change at this time.

Reality Therapy, developed by Dr. William Glasser in 1965, has been used successfully for over twenty-five years to help people gain strength. When used with children, the Reality Therapy model helps them develop personal responsibility. Through a positive, caring, respectful approach we use the questions of Reality Therapy to help children make decisions about their own behavior. We have found that this is much better than a critical approach where children are told what to do but don't learn to think for themselves.

Using Reality Therapy we teach the children that we all have the same basic needs — the need to be loved, the need to be successful, the need to have freedom of choices, and the need for fun. We teach the children and their parents that when they are upset it is because one of their needs is not being met. The children have to figure out for themselves what they need — attention (love), achievement (power), independence (freedom), laughter (fun). When the children learn to do this, instead of being angry or depressed they will have a better behavior. They can ask for what they need instead of being upset. They also can learn to meet their own needs without interfering with other people's needs.

The focus of restitution is an action plan to try a new behavior for a short time and then for the child to evaluate whether or not he has taken a better route. This evaluation is based on how he feels and how he sees that his behavior has affected those around him. This is a technique for developing effective solutions for dealing with painful situations. The educator asks the child the questions of Reality Therapy, and then the child learns to ask himself these questions:

- What do I want?
- What am I doing?
- Is it working? Do I want to change it?
- How can I change it?
- Is this a responsible direction?

We encourage you to teach these questions to your students so they can ask them of each other. The bold print is what the teacher asks the student. If the student doesn't answer, the teacher provides a response of the sort indicated in italics.

1. **What do you want?**
   This is what I need from you.

2. **What are you doing?**
   This is what I see.

3. **Is it working?**
   It's not working.

4. **Do you want to make a plan?**
   This is what I want you to do.

Below are many different ways to phrase the basic questions. The system is very versatile. It does not have to sound like a cookbook.

❶ What do you want?

What's your picture?
What do you want to change?
How do you want your day to be?
Tell me what you want.
What do you want to be thinking?
How do you want to be feeling?
What is your goal?
What do you want to see?
How can I help you get what you want?
What would I say/do?
What brings you in here today?
What is your expectation?
What do you want to hear?
What do you have to have?
What do you want to be saying?
If you had a magic wand, what would you
    change?... ask for?...wish?...see?
What's important to you?
If you could design tomorrow/this afternoon/
    next period, how would it look?
Make this puppet say what "he" wants.
What kinds of choices do you have?
Who do you look up to? Who's your hero? Why?

❷ What are you doing?

What's happening?
What action have you taken?
What happened?
How are you going about it?
What did it look like?
How did it feel?
What worked about it? (evaluate)
What were the steps?
How do you see/perceive it?
Where did it happen?
Where were you/they ...?
What causes that?
What is your body telling you?
What did they do when it happened?
Who was there?
What road are you on?
How hard/loud/soft ...?
What did you say/hear?
How do you think they perceived it?
In what direction are you headed? path?
When did it begin to fall apart?
When did you first ...?
How often have you tried to ...?
What did you see as options?
If I was there, what would I see? Create a picture
    for me!

❸ Is it working?

Is it helping?
How's it going?
Is it cool? (language of the day)
Do you feel good about it?
Are you happy?
Do you like it the way it is?
Are you satisfied?
Are you there yet?
Is it O.K.?
What are the results?
Can you accept the way it is?
Did your plan come together?
Is it better?...or worse?
Are you hurting?
Are you further along than when you started?
Can you get there from here?
Have things improved?
Are you clicking on all four?
Are you getting what you wanted?
Are your needs being met?
Are you doing better?
Are things better?
Do you need to do something differently?
Is your fish bowl full?
Are your ducks in the pond?
Is there wind in your sail?
Is your engine running smoothly?

❹ Do you want to make a plan?

What do you want to do?
What are you going to think?
What will you be thinking/doing?
How could this go better for you?
What would make this more comfortable for you?
What are other ways of looking at this?
What would help?
Who would you be playing with?
Where would you be playing?
When are you going to check in?
What are you going to be saying to yourself?
How are you going to talk to that person?
What words are you going to use?
When are you going to talk to that person?
What will you say?
If ____, what will you think to yourself?
If ____, what will you do?
If ____, what will you say?
What do you need to carry out your plans?
Who do you need to tell?
Do you need some help?
Can I help you with your plan?
If you would like some ideas, I can help you.
Are you going to do it?

Special Situations

I. The Youth Who Says, "I Don't Know."

Teacher: Do you know how to keep going when the going gets rough?

Youth: I don't know.

Teacher: Seriously, when you have trouble in a relationship or in school do you leave it?

Youth: I don't understand.

Teacher: One of the things I noticed is that you started at three schools last year and had four boarding places. You're smart enough to learn in school and you can get along with people, so what is happening? When you run into trouble what do you do?

Youth: Split.

Teacher: That's one way of handling an uncomfortable situation For a while it's a big relief. Now if every time something gets rough you quit, how's it going to work out for you?

Youth: (Shrug) I don't know.

Teacher: Seriously, I'm not criticizing you. I'm not your enemy. Do you know that this is something most people learn at home or on the job or somewhere in life. Did anyone ever teach you this?

Youth: What do you mean?

Teacher: I mean do you have anyone in your family or friends who has had a hard time, say at work or school, and went back and licked it. If you haven't seen this you just haven't had the chance to learn it. Do you know what I'm asking?

Youth: Yeah.

Teacher: Do you believe when I say that this can be learned?

Youth: I don't know.

Teacher gives an example of another student who has learned this and where they learned it in the program.

Teacher: Do you think if we worked together on you learning these things it might go better for you?

Youth: Maybe, I don't know.

Teacher: Would it hurt?

Youth: No, I don't think so.

Teacher: I think you've got a good chance. You know how to learn. You know how to get into programs. There's just this one small thing to work on - staying in.

Youth: Yeah.

Teacher: If you could hang in on this math for the morning, would that be a start?

Youth: Maybe, I don't know.

Teacher: OK, what do you need to do and what do you need to say to yourself to hang in?

Youth: I don't know.

Teacher: What were you saying to yourself a minute ago when you wanted to quit?

Youth: Screw this, I'll never get it right.

Teacher: OK, when you said that to yourself how did you make yourself feel.

Youth: Pissed off.

Teacher: What else?

Youth:	Like a F'ing loser.
Teacher:	So was that good for you?
Youth:	I can't help it.
Teacher:	You're right. You can't help the first thought that jumps up but you can take control of the second one.
Youth:	I don't understand.
Teacher:	Do you want to understand?
Youth:	Why should I?
Teacher:	Because you'll have a lot more power if you can figure out how your brain works.
Youth:	Yeah? Doubt it.
Teacher:	Want to check it out?
Youth:	Go ahead, lay it on me.

II. Counseling the Resistant Child Who Does Not Want to Answer

When counseling the resistant child the staff may have to both ask and answer the questions for awhile. That is alright. It is a stage. The main thing to remember is to take ownership of your own views and avoid using rhetorical questions. Purge your conversation of such rhetorical phrases as:

- You know what the rule is, don't you?
- You weren't where you were supposed to be, were you?
- You know you shouldn't have done that.
- This is important to you isn't it?
- You don't want to fail, do you?
- You want to do better, don't you?

All of these rhetorical questions rob the child of his independence. You are assuming. You don't know. If you use such questions, the child will clam up or may nod in agreement without really assuming any responsibility. It is also essential to avoid pointing, threatening or coercing the child. Therefore in stating a possible negative outcome (e.g. phoning home) use role involvement (e.g. the policy is ..., or it's my job to ...) If you do this the child can't be mad at you personally and is more likely to look at his own behavior.

Not all children are ready for restitution. They do not want to make a plan. They may not even want to answer you. You can pass this test! All you need to do is manage a three-minute interaction without becoming coercive. It doesn't matter if the child changes. If you can resist punishing, laying on guilt, or persuading, the child will need to look at himself. Internal change will take place — even if he isn't answering.

The following are some short examples of the child who does not want to answer you.

1.	Teacher	Child

Teacher	Child
What's the rule?	I don't know.
The rule is ...	I don't care.
Can you do it anyway?	Silence plus non-
Thank you, I appreciate it.	verbal compliance
(Don't hover, move on.)	

2.	Teacher	Child

Teacher	Child
What are you doing?	Nothing.
What I see/hear you doing is ...	Silence
Is it working for you?	Yes.
I understand ... but it's not working for us. We need a better plan. (Wait for the child's answer.)	

3.	Teacher	Child

Teacher	Child
Is this important to you?	Shrug
We want to work this out with you.	Shrug
What we need is for you to ___.	
Can you do that?	Shrug
If you don't we'll have to (consequence)___.	
We don't want to do this.	
Think about it. (Leave the child to sit for a few minutes.)	
Calmly apply the sanction.	Non-compliance.

III. When the Behavior-Disordered Child Comes Into Your Class

A. Mental preparation for the teacher

The following are things you can say to yourself:

- He's doing the best he can. I'm doing the best I can.
- Isn't it interesting how he's trying to control me. What's his need? I'm not going let this work on me.
- It feels so personal but at the same level it has nothing to do with me.
- This kid is lucky to have me!

B. Preliminary work

These are things to be done before the problems are addressed.

- Find out an interest of the child.
- Search the tests to find out a strength, something he can do. (e.g., auditory memory: he can remember words of a popular song or rap.)
- Meet with his parents to collect information on what he can do, his success strategies.

C. The first day of class

Try the following procedure:

- Have a casual conversation before class on a topic which is not about school. It could be held on the play-ground or in the hall.

- Ask him what he'd like to work on that he feels he could be successful at. Give easy options.
- Ask him where he'd like to sit that he thinks he could manage himself. Give choices.
- Ask him how he can signal you, if he needs a break from the group. (Explain to him that your job is to teach the group and ask if he can signal you in a way that doesn't disrupt your teaching. Tell him you'll be over within five minutes.)

D. During class

The following are 'Do's' and 'Don'ts' you may practice:

- Don't hover.
- Don't make a big deal.
- Don't have too many rules.
- Do have him meet with a buddy who will go over the rules with him and whom he can talk to in class at the back.

E. When he misbehaves, as he will

- Say 'I need you to listen.'
- Ask 'Do you need to talk to __(buddy)__?'
- Ask 'Do you need a time out?'
- Ask 'Do you need to go to Mrs. __(counselor)__?
- Ask him to check back with you.

A teacher who had completed her first mainstreaming year said: 'It's been the most rewarding experience of my teaching career. Last year I observed him in his special class and told the principal, 'There's no way I

109

can take this child.' The first month was really cha-
otic. I decided I had to make it work. I would walk him
back to his seat a thousand times if it took a thousand
times. Now when people come into the room they ask
which one is he."

IV. Techniques for Dealing with Smart Aleck Students

Some students who are unsuccessful in meeting their
achievement needs in class like to gain influence by
making sarcastic or rude remarks, usually almost out
of the teacher's hearing. There are a variety of techniques which may be used. Some are listed below.

1. Ignore. If it escalates you'll have to confront.

2. Use humor back (not sarcasm).

3. Say, 'I don't like that; I'd like you to do this instead.'
Redirect the student to a positive activity.

4. Say, 'Pardon me? Could you repeat that? Did I hear
what I thought I heard? What did you say? Care to
rephrase that?"

5. Say, 'I don't talk to you like that."

6. Say, "This is not how you get what you want from
me."

7. Say, 'I need to be teaching you, and this interferes with my ability to help you. Let's get working.'

8. You may decide to say, "Thank you." It can defuse the situation because the affront isn't working.

9. Give a warning of a consequence.

10. As a last resort, invoke a consequence.

A teacher needs to assess which of the above suit her personal style and gear the approach to the individual student. The main things to remember are to be flexible and avoid going toe-to-toe in front of a group of the student's peers.

The real solution to working with this child is to quickly direct him to an activity where he can take some legitimate leadership in order to meet his personal need for power.

V. Shifting to Internal Focus of Control

Most classroom programs have a system of positive reinforcement whereby children gain credits for being on task. This is a system of extrinsic rewards. It tends to erode the intrinsic desire for learning necessary to aid restitution. To help the child shift from conformity to ownership of his actions, and transfer the child from a perceived external locus of control to an internal locus of control, the following steps may be taken. The teacher could say:

1. Do you still need me to give you the check mark, or do you want to give them to yourself when I call time?

2. Do you need ten check marks every ten minutes, or will one be enough if one is worth the same as ten were previously worth?

3. Can you watch the clock and give yourself a check mark when you've been on task for ten minutes? thirty minutes? a class period? a morning?

4. Do you still need the check marks, or can you work for a morning without them? What I want is to give you the reward without the check marks. Do you think you can handle it? Do you need my help? A reminder?

As we extinguish the token economy it is essential to build up the internal strength. Ask the child:

5. For what would you like to give yourself a check mark for this morning that took effort for you to do?

6. For what do you want to be recognized by the group?

7. Do we still need the check marks or could we just keep the recognition process (turtle points, etc.)?

8. Do you still need us to recognize what you're doing well or can you do it for yourself?

9. Suppose I don't believe what you did took effort? Whose opinion counts? Who really knows the answer?

10. What do you think you could offer others to help them learn? Will you do it?

11. What recognition would you want from others, if any?

12. Is what you're doing now getting you what you want?

Such a series of questions can over a period of two weeks help a child to develop confidence in his own ability. He will test you. He will want you to give your opinion. If you do so, be clear that it is only your opinion. You are not him. You will not be following him in the world. He is the decision maker in his life!

VI. Trial by Fire: The Substitute Teacher

Twice this year in my visits to quality schools, the substitute teacher sent back a message to a teacher in the training. The message ran something as follows: 'Your class was a pleasure to be with. They came in, took out their projects and independently worked until recess asking for help as they needed it.' In one case the teacher added, 'The only problem was they wanted to stay in at recess and do their research projects.' Even more amazing was the other substitute teacher who added, 'I feel guilty taking my money.'

I listened to these stories, delighted that the class teachers were getting what they wanted in the way of self-evaluation and independent quality work. I reflected back on my experiences as a substitute teacher. Believe me, I never felt guilty taking my money! In fact, of any position I worked in a school, this one was the hardest to master. Why was this? Upon reflection I realize that putting a substitute teacher in a class is a situation designed for the definition of limits.

In 1983, when I was teaching in the College of Education, I decided that if I were going to be training teachers I had best keep my skills honed. I put myself on the substitute teachers list with the school board and soon an opportunity arose — a replacement for a vice principal-teacher working with a Grade Seven class in the morning and a Grade Eight class in the afternoon. In the morning I did everything that I knew from experience would help me. I reviewed the teacher's lesson plan and set up a slide projector for the science lesson. I put the questions on the board and checked the seating chart. Then I lingered at the door chatting to the students and I showed interest in the work on the wall of the school until the bell rang.

For the first ten or fifteen minutes I had their attention as they took their measure of me. Did I know the rules? How strict was I? Could they manipulate me? Then they struck deftly, each playing his or her part as if orchestrated. 'Can I go to the washroom? Can I sit with Rebecca? Do we have to do Science? Could we do Art? Can we listen to the radio? Mr. Hart lets us. Mr. Hart says we can do what we want. Do we have to take notes? I don't have an ink pen. I can't see from here; can I move to the back? I can't see from the back; can I move to the front? I left my sweater outside; can I go out and get it? My hands are all dirty; can I please wash them first? Eric's feet are too stinky. I'll switch places with Carmen. She says she can't smell 'cause she has a bad cold."

Listening to these demands I felt myself slipping into a reactive mode. I began to attempt to field their questions. As I did so, my vision of my purpose in this classroom became more and more remote. Finally I was not teaching but surviving the barrage as I dog-paddled to noon hour. At one point, I put on the slide projector and gained an additional 10 minutes of attention, but even then there was an intermittent buzzing between desks.

At noon I decided to take action. My next class was Grade Eight Social Studies. I went to the office and asked the principal, "What's the worst thing I can do if they don't listen?" He replied, "Mr. Hart always has them multiply a six-digit number by itself. The first offense they square it; the second, they cube it; and so forth." "How long does this go on?" I asked. "Forever," he said, "Usually some students are finishing it in detention." "Oh," I replied, " Thank you for the technique," and I sat down to decide what to do.

I made my plan. After recess I greeted the new group of students as they filed in. I decided I was going to utilize my ten minutes of grace. I began by telling them my name. I told them I had been informed of the multiplication consequence and would use it if necessary, but that I would prefer to work out with them how the afternoon would go. I said, "Let's take the first 10 minutes for a class meeting," and I formed them into a circle. I asked, "What is a substitute teacher?" "How am I different from a regular teacher?" "How do you behave with a substitute teacher?" "Why is that?" "What are the advantages of a substitute teacher?" "The disadvantages?" "What do you think my job is in here?" At that point, I let them know what I thought my job was. "My job," I said, "is to supervise your Social Studies class in a way so there is no noise in the hall if anyone is walking by. Your teacher says you have your projects on which to work. I don't care where you sit or with whom you work with if you can cooperate and get your work done. I'm the person to whom you can pose questions. I'm the person who has to keep it safe in here. Can you figure out what to do from there? Can you do it quietly? Do I have to use the multiplication or can you do it on your own?"

They asked a couple of questions of clarification, then they began. Most of them chose to work with someone. They all worked on their projects. Several times I was asked questions. I put one boy in the hall after asking him, "Can you study better out there without any distractions?" Halfway through, I turned on the radio and there was soft background music. I had a beautiful afternoon. I felt my pay check had been easily earned.

Within a single day I had two very different experiences. I now realize, in light of my knowledge of Quality School management, why the second approach was more comfortable. It elicited more learning because it was less coercive. Also in the second situation I knew my bottom line and announced it before the students needed to push to find the limits.

What has this experience to offer a teacher who is either new to a class or a temporary replacement for the regular teacher? I suggest the following:

1. Do something very different to start with to get the students' attention and throw them out of their old pattern.

2. Redefine the role of the substitute teacher using My Job Is/My Job Is Not.

3. Let them know that you know the bottom line.

4. Focus on the joint task to be accomplished by the group with you. (power need)

5. Set minimal conditions and maximize choices. (freedom need)

6. Allow them to work cooperatively if conditions are met. (belonging need)

7. Use humor and have fun with the class. As much as possible, be yourself. (fun need)

8. If you are a new teacher beginning a class, I advise you to start with a few class rules and suggest that the group review them in two weeks. That way they will have chance to get used to you and you to them first.

By following as many of these guidelines as possible, one can make the experience of being a substitute teacher satisfying for both students and teacher.

Summary

This chapter deals with the questions of Reality Therapy and how to use them in working with difficult students. The questions are:

- What do you want? What's the rule?
- What are you doing? saying?
- Is it working? Is it against the rule?
- Can you figure out a better way?

Several examples have been given to illustrate how to apply the principles of management to disciplining difficult students.

When To Do What

1. When should I say "YES IF...?"

- When there *is* a choice.
- When the child is asking for permission and the teacher can use discretion.

- The "if" states a condition that is possible for the child.
- If you say "no" state the reason.

2. When should I ask "WHAT'S YOUR JOB HERE?" or "WHAT DO YOU NEED TO BE DOING HERE?" or "WHAT DID WE AGREE ON?"

- When talking about the child's or teacher's responsibility or their job in the class.
- The teacher has already previously outlined this with the class.

3. When should I ask "WHAT'S THE RULE? CAN YOU DO THAT?"

- When it's a discipline situation.
- When the children know the rule.
- When a change is necessary and the teacher needs to enforce the rule.

4. When should I ask "WHAT ARE YOU DOING?"

- When the child is unaware of what he's doing.
- If you need information or facts.
- If the child doesn't answer, be prepared to give the facts as you see them.

5. When should I ask "WHAT DO YOU WANT?" or "WHAT DO YOU NEED?"

- When the child is upset and you don't understand why. "What is it you're not getting that you are so upset.

6. When should I say "HOW WOULD YOU LIKE IT TO BE?" or "HOW WOULD YOU LIKE TO HANDLE THIS?"

- When the child is complaining and telling you what he doesn't want.
- When the child is talking about what the other person is doing to him.

"Teaching kids to count is fine,
but teaching them what counts
is best."

— *Bob Talbert*

Chapter Six

Making It Right

Restitution does not happen in a vacuum. Restitution is the product of the interrelationship of three variables: the person I want to be, my social conscience or how I want to be treated by others, and the value to be protected.

It is impossible to get anything other than conformity if the child cannot understand the effect of his actions on others. For example, a two-year-old is hitting his brother with a block. If he doesn't make the connection between his brother crying and what he did, he is too young for the practice of restitution. Also if he doesn't understand the value at stake — in this case it would be "We don't hurt other people" or "Treat others as you would like to be treated" — he can't make restitution. Therefore in the school before a restitution can be practiced the child will need to want to be part of the group. He will also need to be educated as to the values held by the group. Thirdly, he will need to make the decision that he wants to be a person who is caring and who is strong enough to repair his mistakes.

In our society we have recognized the importance of these variables but have often taught them while in the punishing or guilting mode so that when the child compared his behavior with the goal he felt like a bad person. The tone of voice is all important in asking the following questions: "What do we believe in our classroom about how we treat each other?" or "What do we believe in our classroom about replacing another's property?" Then we need to ask, "Are you the kind of person who treats others with respect?" or "Are you the kind of person who can make restitution when you make a mistake?" I have also found it useful to intermittently ask the question, "Are you the kind of person who can follow through on what you say you'll do?" The tone in each of these questions is direct and interested in the answer while not attempting to control the outcome. These questions teach children that we are not searching for fault, we are searching for a remedy. We are interested in the kind of person they are becoming.

The pursuit of restitution is a creative art. The answer as to what is to be done is not always immediately clear. In order to practice restitution one must remain focused on what one wants to achieve. Our first goal is the strengthening of the child who has offended, for if we allow him to sit in his offense then we allow him to slip into failure. Our second goal is compensation to the person wronged. This gives the class a strong message about the potential of our classroom to be a need-satisfying environment for them. The form of the restitution is where we can practice our creativity.

It is the job of the teacher to frame up the restitution on the positive side with both our needs and the child's needs in mind using questions such as, 'What could you do to give back to the class some of the time you have used up without having to miss the after school activity?' or 'How could you repay him without looking like a wimp?' or 'What could you do to repair that broken equipment that won't cost your dad money?' Often children will initially answer, 'It's not possible,' because they do not see an immediate solution. However, if we are patient, ask the question again, frame up the conditions, and give them some time, they are generally able to come up with an idea. This process assists children in developing the kind of thinking necessary for the 21st century where the problems they encounter will be multi-faceted.

If they can't come up with a suggestion then we can offer a possibility. Usually when there is difficulty with a solution it is because we are looking too concretely and focusing on the offense rather than focusing on strengthening the child and providing an opportunity for him to contribute to us, the group.

A key aspect to remember when questioning is the importance of allowing the child time to think on his own to make a decision and then to find a restitution. The process of restitution is an invitation not a demand. It cannot be rushed. The following stories describe real-life situations where restitution was used effectively.

The Wayward Trio

A group of us had taken our grade seven students camping last June. The theme for our outing revolved around cooperation and problem solving. During co-operative games a head count revealed we were short three students. Fifteen seconds later a couple of the girls were volunteering how these missing three had decided it would be more fun to stay in their tent and chat. So...up the grassy slope I trudged. Sure enough the giggles directed me to the trio. I asked them to come out and then directed my delinquents to the now famous picnic table. As the kids quoted, 'If you're in-vited for a chat at the picnic table, they mean busi-ness.' I explained to the girls that this was a coopera-tive camp and asked if they had demonstrated coop-eration. They indicated 'no.' Further discussion led to other observations such as, 'We should have been there, we didn't realize anyone would miss us, etc.' I asked them to talk together and see if they could come up with a plan. This plan was to reflect cooperation and sharing. As I explained to the girls, the other youngsters who were down playing the games had lost out. They had been denied the quality my trio would have added to the group.

I left leaving the girls to their task. I sat down within eyesight but not hearing range. Body language said it all! Initially they were stiff and formal but then movement started. I could sense they were on to some-thing but I continued to sit patiently. It didn't take more than ten minutes. They ended up sitting on the picnic table, laughing and giggling, so over I went.

Their plan was to teach the group a new game, one they had learned elsewhere, not in school. It was obvious one of the girls had become the leader but the other two indicated they felt confident and that they understood how to play this game too. So...off we went.

As we approached the group I could hear those famous 'Oh, ohs.' The gym teacher asked everyone to sit down and you could see they were waiting for the lecture. I simply explained that the girls had been busy preparing an activity for the large group and that they'd like to share it. So, the trio took over. They explained, modeled, organized, and implemented. It was great! The group was happy and complimented the trio about the new fun game. The trio was back in the group and they were smiling too.

The Guest Reader

I have several "challenges" in my class but one particular boy has really lead me to delve into restitution. One of my objectives with him has been to get him to come out of his shell and expose a bit of himself. Punishment would defeat this objective.

He was being particularly stubborn and uncooperative one day, delaying the lesson by about five to ten minutes with his antics. So, off he and I went to our conference room. I explained that as class manager I found it unacceptable when people deliberately sabotaged our progress and asked what he could do to remedy the situation. He sat and fiddled. Finally, he admitted he didn't know what to do.

It was quite early in the school year and I didn't know this lad well, but I had observed that when we went to the library he really enjoyed browsing through the books and always selected what I'd term a "neat book." I found this fascinating because reading was difficult for him and he'd avoid it if possible. I led the conversation at this point and asked him what library book he had in his desk. He told me. Further discussion revealed that he had not really read the book, but that he felt he could if he practiced and that he was confident the class would enjoy it. So I asked if he would consent to reading to the class to entertain them for ten minutes giving back the lost time. He was fascinating to watch because his eyes and body became alive. He wanted to know if that was all he had to do. We struck a deal; he'd do it the next day as a surprise. So that afternoon as I dismissed, I wrote on the board that our class was going to have a "guest reader" come in and entertain us tomorrow. It doesn't take much to arouse the curiosity of ten- and eleven-year-olds. As he left, I noticed the book tucked under his arm.

The next day during class I slid an empty desk in the front of the room and gave my boy a build up without revealing who was going to read. Sure enough, he pulled out the book and sauntered up. The reading was slow, jerky, and labored, but he read. His audience was appreciative and complimented him. I gave a sigh of relief. After that, we had "guest readers" daily. Notes were dropped on my desk all covered with Scotch tape so they'd be private, and everyone tried to guess who was going to entertain that day. My boy continued to appear as a "guest reader" as well.

An offshoot of this led to a group of boys who were in trouble writing a short skit and then performing their work for the class. I viewed this exercise as a success too. They got positive attention from their peers and obviously felt very good about themselves.

The Bicycle Caper

Two girls, sisters in fact, wanted revenge against a certain boy, so just prior to the beginning of school at lunch time they went into the bicycle area and let out the air from the boy's tires. They were very proud of their accomplishment except for a couple of things. They had targeted the wrong bike and one of our teachers had watched the entire incident from her window which overlooks the bike area. The principal took them into the conference area and the games began.

Classes started and my girl wasn't in class. Later, she was still not in class. Eventually, I had a short break and went looking. My principal was still locked up with the two in the conference room, and even though I couldn't hear the conversation, body language told who was winning. He came out when he saw me and declared, 'I can't even get them to admit it, never mind about fixing it!" I asked if I could try, and he said, "Be my guest."

Ten minutes later, there was a plan. The girls were to help the lad get his bike over to the garage on the corner. There, they would assist him to put air into his tires and help check to see the pressure was correct. We approached the boy and he agreed, and the three decided to meet in the school yard at dismissal time.

I felt the reason the girls cooperated with me was because I avoided the issue of admitting guilt. My chat with them consisted of, "Okay, you're in a situation here, how are we going to rectify it?" They took it from there.

The Clean-Up Detail

While the whole school was doing clean-up of the outside area, two fourth grade boys came into the school without permission. Their teacher has had considerable trouble with these boys as they usually try to get out of doing things with various excuses. The teacher brought the two boys to my office and it went like this.

Principal: "Boys, it looks like you did something you know is wrong. How can you make up for this?

The two boys sat there blankly as if to say, "We've done nothing, what do you mean?

'My next question was, "Well, boys, I know Ms. X is quite upset with you two coming into the school without permission. Is there some way that you can make up so that she feels okay about it and you know that you feel okay about it?"

Boys: "How?"

Principal: "Well, we call it restitution. That means making up for something you've done that was wrong. Is there something you can think of that you might be able to do?"

Ricky: "Well, maybe we could clean up some more."

Principal: "That sounds like a good idea. So, when could you clean up?"

Ricky: "Tomorrow."

Principal: "When tomorrow?"
One boy says recess, the other one says after school, and so neither can go at the same time. My question was: "Well, boys, how's Wednesday after school?

Boys: "Fine, for how long?"

Principal: "How long do you think?"

Boys: "We don't know. Oh, about half an hour."

Principal: "I'll designate the area. Okay, boys?"

Boys: "But we got to be home straight after school."

Principal: "Well, then, today can you let your mother know that you are doing a job for Mr. Williams from 2:30 to 3:00 on Wednesday?"

Boy: "Yes, I can."

Principal: "Fine, boys. I'll see you Wednesday after school for your clean-up. How do you feel about that?"

Boys: "Fine."

Principal: "Okay, now will you tell Ms. X that you've come up with a restitution?"

Boys: "Yeah."

Principal: "Can you remember the word?"

Boys: "Yes, sir."

Principal: "Fine, you let her know and then tell Ms. X to talk to me about it so that I know that you have told her. Okay, boys, back to class now."

Improving Attendance

Tumwater High School's staff expects punctual, regular attendance. Over the past years the staff has developed several attendance policies in order to raise student attendance. Even though student attendance is consistently above 90%, they continue to be concerned with attendance and its correlation to learning. Many traditional programs have been used such as detention, work detail, and suspension. In the spring of 1991 the staff again examined student attendance with the additional knowledge base of Dr. William Glasser's books *The Quality School* and *Control Theory*. The process for new policy development was a collaborative effort by the entire staff Committee work set the initial framework for the policy and procedures and an in-service day was used to involve other staff members in modification and finalization. The policy was designed to educate those students who were experiencing difficulty in making responsible decisions concerning their attendance. The staff also examined the curriculum and teaching methodology to make learning more valuable and to create a more need-satisfying environment for students. The main elements in the educational program they developed consisted of:

1. Group intervention with students which is facilitated by a counselor or administrator. This intervention occurs during the school day at a time designed for students to receive additional classroom assistance, do correctives, and/or enrichment (approximately 30 minutes). The focus of this intervention is to teach the

students about the basic human needs and a responsible way in which to satisfy them.

2. Group seminar with students which is facilitated by a staff member. This seminar occurs after school (approximately 2 hours) and consists of extended teaching of 'Control Theory.' The emphasis of the seminar includes:

A. Human needs
B. Total behavior model (acting, thinking, feeling, and physiology)
C. Development of a plan for behavior change

Procedures were developed and agreed upon by the staff for the use of the interventions and seminars. The following are steps that a staff member would use when initiating the process for a student referral into the educational program.

If truancy becomes a factor in a student's success, the following sequenced guidelines may be used at the teacher's discretion:

A. Intervention with the student and parent contact.
B. Refers student for initial intervention.
C. Refers student for after-school seminar.
D. Further truancy may lead to the removal of student from class.

If the student develops a chronic tardy problem the teacher may follow similar steps as for truancies.

This attendance program was the first attempt to solve student attendance problems through an educational format instead of developing additional means of punishment. It has only recently been initiated so there are no statistics yet on changes in student attendance patterns, although several group interventions have been used and the immediate results have been positive. The students that are involved in the interventions have developed some changes in attendance patterns and have consistently asked for more information on meeting their needs and on their behavioral system.

Moving Toward Restitution

I believe those of you who read this are working diligently to avoid punishing children. Most of us are aware when we are tempted to resort to physical punishment and consciously change our practices. However, are you aware of the guilt your voice may convey or the persuasion you use to convince a student? This is not easy. As teachers each of us needs to examine our own discipline practices. Do we harbor the illusion we can make others conform? Do we believe it is our responsibility to coerce? Or do we accept that each individual has the right to free choice providing he doesn't interfere with other's meeting their needs? I have been using ideas in this book for two decades and still, to this day, hear myself posing questions that are controlling rather than eliciting. Awareness is the first step.

This book has focused on methods for less coercive classroom management. The concept of restitution has been presented as an approach to strengthen children. It is offered in place of punishment and monitoring as a vehicle for children to develop self-discipline. It is a collaborative process which teaches children to seek solutions to problems. The emphasis on values reminds the child not only of his rights but of his obligations to the social contract. The focus of the change we ask the students to make is rooted in his self-examination of the person he wants to become. The process of restitution taps the higher self, the altruistic self. It moves the child from avoiding discomfort to building quality into his interactions with others. It is proactive.

When I hear myself cajoling, creating guilt, or threatening, I pose another question in an even tone that is direct. For instance, if I hear myself say, 'Didn't you say you'd finish that paper last night?', I change the form of the question to, "What was your plan when you left last night?" I also change my tone to one that is respectful and questioning. Learning to question honestly without intent takes enormous self-discipline. About two-thirds of the time I accomplish this in my initial interaction. The other third of the time I correct myself and refocus the interaction away from fault-finding.

Remind yourself that it took a long time to learn your current patterns of interaction; you don't have to reverse them overnight. Use the following pages as tools for self-assessment on the techniques outlined in this book. The first checklist is a quick survey to identify how frequently the interaction is being used by the teacher. The second is a checklist to evaluate school-based practices. The third is a checklist a teacher can use to help students evaluate whether they are solution-oriented. The fourth tool is a checklist to monitor statements both ineffective and effective that you as a teacher might say out loud or to yourself. The fifth form includes questions teachers can use to get meetings back on track. The sixth form is a list devised by a group of teachers after one week of practicing the ideas of less coercive management toward restitution. Use it to give yourself ideas as to how you might begin.

I. Teacher Checklist

On the following scale, rank how often you do each of
the following. 1-Never, 2-Rarely, 3-Sometimes, 4-Often.

A. Classroom Techniques

1. "My job is / Your job is"   1 2 3 4

2. "Yes if"   1 2 3 4

3. Asking, "What's the rule?
   Can you do that?"   1 2 3 4

4. Offering the student a
   restitution option.
   (Figure out what you can do.)   1 2 3 4

5. Saying, "That won't work"
   (with regard to controlling
   emotional behavior)   1 2 3 4

6. With complaints asking,
   "How would you like it to be?"   1 2 3 4

7. Use of time out options and
   two-way communication with
   principal on these   1 2 3 4

8. Class expectations and values   1 2 3 4

9. Teaching and asking children
   about their needs   1 2 3 4

10. After an intervention,
    analyzing whether it was
    discipline or punishment   1 2 3 4

B. Personal Applications

1. Aware of my personal
   needs and the needs of others   1 2 3 4

2. Aware of and modifying
   tone of voice or nonverbal   1 2 3 4
   gestures

3. Saying things to take the
   pressure off (e.g. I'm doing   1 2 3 4
   the best I can. It's okay
   to make a mistake.)

4. Reframing negative "killer
   statements" to the positive side   1 2 3 4

5. Aware of my bad feeling
   signals and my own needs   1 2 3 4

6. Stating my needs to others
   rather than complaining   1 2 3 4

7. Doing something for myself
   to lower my stress level   1 2 3 4

II. How Do We Know Restitution is Being Practiced in this Organization?

Check which of the following is true in your school.

___ 1. There is no blame, only 'making it right' through restitution. Fault is not an issue. People look for solutions rather than focusing on problems.

___ 2. There is a low level of complaining.

___ 3. There is a lot of laughter.

___ 4. People like their jobs.

___ 5. People see themselves more as the same than different from those they help.

___ 6. People encourage each other.

___ 7. People state what they need.

___ 8. People use role involvement and are consistent in enforcement of rules.

___ 9. Students know the rules and have input to the rules.

___ 10. Most of the energy is put into projects and activities on the positive side.

___ 11. Administrators visit and socialize with staff and have some direct involvement with the students.

___ 12. Students know and talk about the aims of the program and their personal goals. They're proud.

___ 13. Not much time needs to be spent on discipline.

___ 14. You can't tell the difference between staff and students in terms of responsibility. Both practice responsible behavior.

___ 15. Both teachers and students enjoy coming to school.

III. How You Know the Students are Moving Toward Restitution

1. The students can describe their behavior. They know the difference between facts and their opinions about the facts.

What were you doing when he did what he did?

What were you saying? How were you saying it?

Also, they can answer factual questions. When, where, who, how long, how hard, how many times, etc.

2. They can make evaluations, choices, and decisions. Examples:
    *   Is this working for you? (*No*)
    *   Is this helping you to pass Science? (*No*)
    *   If you keep on doing half of a lesson a day, will you finish by the end of May? (*No*)
    *   Is it important to you to finish by the end of May? (*Yes*)
    *   Do you want to figure out a way to get these lessons done? (*Yes*)

3. They have short-term plans. They know their plans. They talk about their daily plans during the program. They are receptive to reminders or jokes about their plans.

4. They have long-term goals that they perceive as need-fulfilling. They can articulate their goals and relate their plans to their goals if questioned.

5. They are learning to make and to keep short-term commitments.

6. They develop probability determination skills. They understand that there are positive consequences to doing their plan. They also understand that not doing their plan can have negative consequences.

> If you are able to complete your plan, how will it
> be better for you?
> If you don't do this, what will happen?

7. They understand and follow the rules because they are involved in the program. They accept discipline in the form of making restitution, replanning, or short-term exclusion from the group until they are ready to change.

8. They understand that different people can have different points of view. Each person's view is valid. They have learned to say, "The way I see it is ..." or "My opinion is different from yours," or "I hear it a little differently," etc.

9. They understand the principle of restitution and can figure out how to remedy mistakes.

IV. Effective vs. Ineffective Teachers

Effective teachers ask the following:

- What do we need to figure out? (our contract)
- How would you like it to be?
- What specifically do you want to be hearing or seeing from me or us?
- What did we agree on? What's the rule? Can you do that? Thank you.
- How did you handle yourself? What did you do? What did you say?
- What are you doing? Is it working?
- How are you thinking about it? Can you change that? Will you change it? When will you do it?
- That won't work here; figure out another way.

Ineffective Teachers:

- Avoid controversy and discussion.
- Emphasize the right answer.
- Give lots of homework.
- Test frequently.
- Tailor courses to tests.
- Are impersonal.
- Threaten or coerce.
- Say, "It won't work."
- Say, "This family is the same with all their kids."
- Say, "I don't have the time."
- Say, "I can't do it for everyone."
- Say, "He needs a counselor. I can't help him."
- Say, "It's nothing new. We've tried it before."

V. Restitution in the Staff Meeting

We can use the principles of restitution on ourselves as well as on our students. Sometimes when meetings are deteriorating, we ask why it's not working instead of figuring out a way to make it right. If we focus on our goals rather than on the problems, we can be much more efficient with regard to meeting time.

The following are some questions for teachers to ask themselves to move a meeting in a positive direction.

Is this getting us where we want to be?
What's our goal here?
Are we still on the problem?
Can we move to the solution?
What are we shooting for?
What can we do?
What's your plan?
What's your suggestion?
What do we want out of this?
Where do we want to be by 4:00?
What do we need to have figured out by the end of
    this meeting?
Is this under our control?
Do we want to spend this much time on something
    we can't change?
What can we control here?
Can we think about this differently?
Is everyone participating?
What can we do to encourage participation?
How am I participating?
Am I talking too much?

Is saying nothing going to get me what I want?

Am I listening? Do I understand the person's need?

Am I being silent, then complaining about the
   outcome later?

Where are we on the levels? (Don't want, Do want
   or the Plan?)

What's your picture?

Are we into personal issues here?

I also recommend to large groups that they designate a person who's job for a specific meeting is to use this list of questions. Whenever a meeting is going off track, this staff person's job is to ask one of these questions. It is quite a bit of fun and really cuts down on complaining. Rotate the role through different staff members so each gets practice with the process. Eventually the role will become obsolete.

VI. What You Can Do In Your Classroom

Ask, "What's the rule?"

Repeat the rule.

Review the rules with the class.

Review the consequences with class.

Do "My Job/Your Job "with the class.

Ask, "Can you do that?"

Ask, "What do you want? Why is it important?"

Reach an individual by talking to the group.

Talk to parents, focusing on the child's needs.

Talk about something other than the problem.

Do something with the child instead of talking.

Use "Yes if ..." I'm aware of saying "No" so often.
Ask them to tell you what they need.
Use "I need you to ..."
Use "Yes if ..."
Touch a child and say, "People make mistakes; now
　　what can you do?"
Ask, "What do you need to be doing?"
Ask, when they tattle, "Is that your job?" They know
　　the answer.
Stop saying "No."

Summary

Approach restitution with the following philosophical
tenets:

• Everyone makes mistakes. Mistakes are normal; to
err is the human condition.

• People know when they have done wrong.
Even a child understands when he has broken something or hurt someone.

• Guilt and criticism contribute to defensive behavior.
People put up walls and use a lot of energy
rationalizing past wrongs to preserve their self-esteem
when under attack.

• People can learn a better way if we can keep them
on the success side. If we can view them as capable, re-

sponsible, and willing to change even in the face of their mistake, they have incentive to move forward.

• People are strengthened by the opportunity to make restitution. Because everyone makes mistakes, an important life skill is learning to repair them.

• People won't lie or hide their mistakes if they believe they are capable of making restitution and will be given an opportunity.

• The process of making restitution is a creative one which builds problem-solving skills in the offender.

• People who have been allowed to make restitution are generous with others who make mistakes. They are non-punitive themselves as adults.

"There is no adequate defense,
except stupidity,
against the impact
of a new idea.**"**
— *Percy W. Bridgman*

Readings

Glasser, William, *Reality Therapy*. New York: HarperCollins, 1969.

Glasser, William, *Stations of the Mind*. New York: HarperCollins, 1981.

Glasser, William, *Control Theory: A New Explanation of How We Control Our Lives*. New York: HarperCollins, 1984.

Glasser, William, *The Quality School: Managing Students Without Coercion*. New York: HarperCollins, 1990.

Good, E. Perry, *In Pursuit of Happiness*. Chapel Hill: New View Publications, 1987.

Good, E. Perry, *Helping Kids Help Themselves*. Chapel Hill: New View Publications, 1992.

McFadden, Judy, *The Simple Way to Raise a Good Kid*. Sydney, Australia: Horowitz Grahame, PTY Ltd., 1988.

Sullo, Robert A., *Teach Them to Be Happy*. Chapel Hill: New View Publications, 1989.

Powers, William T., *Behavior: The Control of Perception*. Chicago: Aldine Publishing Co., 1973.

Wubbolding, Robert E., *Using Reality Therapy*. New York: HarperCollins, 1988.

Wubbolding, Robert E., *Understanding Reality Therapy*. New York: HarperCollins, 1991.

About The Author

Diane Chelsom Gossen is a senior faculty member of the Institute for Reality Therapy. She has taught the ideas of Reality Therapy and Control Theory for the past twenty years throughout Canada, the United States, Europe, and Australia. She has served on the faculty of several universities, including the University of Saskatchewan and Brandon University and has done training for a broad range of school-based programs. Diane Chelsom Gossen was the founder and, for eight years, the director of the Radius Tutoring Project in Saskatchewan and has been both a trainer and training supervisor for the Saskatchewan Department of Justice, the Saskatchewan Alcohol and Drug Abuse Commission and numerous public and private drug rehabilitation centers, community centers, and correctional facilities.